FRESHWATER
Fishing

FRESHWATER

Fishing

TECHNIQUES & EQUIPMENT FOR SUCCESSFUL SPORT FISHING

Edited by Barrie Rickards

SMITHMARK

CONTENTS

INTRODUCTION

Predatory fish are in some respects the finest and most fascinating of all fish. A trout has no rival for elegance. The lightning lunge of a pike is without equal in the natural world. To understand what aquatic predation is all about, you need to have seen perch herding young fry into the bank: the victims dart around on the surface, leaping in panic and often falling back onto dry land, where other, winged, predators await them. Game fish are also most difficult to catch. It is not enough to present them with the right bait; it must appear to have life, to behave like a crippled fish. Whether or not it is edible does not matter, attracted by the right vibration, they will go for a metal spoon or a wet fly made from fur and feather.

This exciting and challenging sport is drawing more and more devotees. The Americans have shown the way. With no traditions to maintain, they have invented "vibration-making devices," complex baits combining revolving pieces of metal, undulating paddles, and flexible lures.

This book describes how you can catch these fish by a variety of traditional and new methods. The magnificent photographs in this book, taken by an American team, show you the secret life of the game fish and from observing its behavior and beauty your respect for it will grow. It is a worthy adversary.

As we had such exceptional photographs, we invited some exceptional fishermen to tell you about "their" fish, to recount their experiences, and to let you share their enthusiasm in their own individual style.

Barrie Rickards (editor) is an academic by profession and an angler for pleasure. Although fishing for pike is his speciality, he devotes much of his time to promoting the sport through his books, articles, TV and radio appearances; his membership of angling organizations and his concern for the proper use of water resources. Barrie has also contributed a section on fishing for static deadbait.

Jacques Chavanne writes about perch. A teacher by profession, he also writes for angling magazines on his specialist subject. For over thirty years he has been pursuing game fish at least three days a week—more when he can escape his classes.

Pierre Affre is a veterinarian and an expert on fish. A most accomplished angler, he also speaks from worldwide experience. His theme is the fish dearest to his heart: the pike. He has fished for it in American waters as well as in Scandinavia and throughout France.

Henri Limouzin is a knowledgeable and entertaining writer on the art of angling. He was one of the first to hunt the zander, close kin to the walleye. A great enthusiast for the sport, he has done much to popularize game-fishing techniques.

Marc Sourdot is an academic too but spends his spare time on the river bank. His main quarry is the salmon, which he has pursued all over the world, especially in Norway, where he spends his summers. A confirmed fly-fisherman, he also fishes for trout and other game fish.

Gilbert Bordes is a writer. Since early childhood he has fished for wild trout and there is little he does not know about this noble fish.

Yvan Drachkovitch is a most enthusiastic walleye or zander fisherman. But, true angler that he is, he is eager to fish for other game fish—pike, perch, and trout. Devoted to the extent of fishing over three hundred days a year, he is familiar with most fishing grounds.

OXYGEN

Predatory fish are the most demanding of oxygen. Oxygen in the air dissolves in the water on contact, which explains why cold, fast-flowing rivers have the highest oxygen content, while spring waters tend to be poorest in this vital element. Aquatic plants also contribute significantly, by photosynthesis, to the oxygen supply.

WATER

Where does fresh water come from? Seas and oceans cover four fifths of the surface of the planet, and a process of evaporation is going on continuously. Winds are instrumental in carrying humid air toward the land masses, where it condenses on rising. Rain falls to the earth, some filters through the surface strata and forms reservoirs of ground water, which overflow in the form of springs. Other water runs directly into streams. These sources supply lakes, streams and rivers, which return the water to the sea, beginning the cycle all over again, season by season.

The chemical properties and temperature of fresh water supplies depend on the various soil and rock formations they flow through. These factors determine the plant and animal life a given body of water will support and hence the abundance or scarcity of predatory fish, which are the final link in the food chain.

Eutrophication. This lake is over-rich in organic nutrients, causing prolific algae and plant growth. Photosynthesis can take place only on the surface, the oxygen supply is severely depleted, and fish can die in large numbers.

PLANT LIFE

Spring water is generally poor in organic matter. It is, therefore, not always a fertile biological medium and may support few living organisms. Phytoplankton need nutrients in the form of nitrogenous salts if a food chain is to be established. Nutrients of this kind are washed into lakes and rivers by rainwater running off the land. They bring fertility but, in excess, can cause serious pollution problems. When algae and aquatic plants proliferate beyond a certain point, they deprive fish of their vital oxygen supplies. The first hint of problems is usually an excess of blanket weed.

TEMPERATURE

Each species of fish grows and reproduces within a certain temperature range. Cold-water species, such as members of the salmon tribe, thrive in mountain lakes and in the higher reaches of rivers. They have a very high oxygen requirement. Another category of fish prefer more temperate waters. Pike and perch, for instance, can stand low temperatures but are also at home in warmer summer conditions. Warm-water species prefer the lower reaches of rivers, where the longest and most productive food chains develop. Fish of this kind, particularly members of the carp family, survive in poorly oxygenated waters, where their numbers are controlled by predators such as the pike and the walleye.

A lake in the far north of Quebec province. Although such cold habitats produce few nutrients, the large amount of dissolved oxygen in the water is favorable to such demanding fish as trout and char.

FISH MOVEMENTS THROUGH THE SEASONS

Predatory fish depend just as much on season and water temperature as the bait fish on which they feed. Predators which lurk, like the pike, or actively seek out their prey, like the perch and walleye, must inhabit the same areas as their victims. Knowing how shoals of bait fish move around seasonally enables the angler to find a good spot.

Movements of this kind are particularly marked in deep lakes of the kind formed by a dam. Similar movements can be observed in natural lakes, especially if there are deep trenches where cold-sensitive members of the carp family tend to take refuge in winter and fish such as the trout seek relief from the summer heat.

SPRING

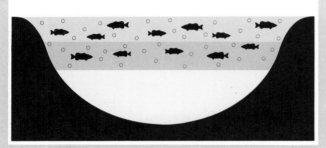

Early spring. The ice, if present, begins to melt and the sun, gaining strength, warms up the surface of the water. Stirred by the wind, this warm layer becomes rich in oxygen. The fish rise to the surface, preferring to remain in the shallows.

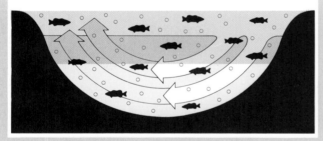

Mid-spring. The whole mass of water attains the same temperature. As the wind pushes the surface water, it sets up counter-currents which carry oxygen down into the depths. The fish swim at all levels.

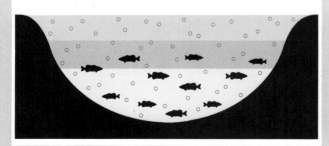

Late spring. Fish, other than salmon and trout, seek out warm water in which to breed. Though well oxygenated, the lower levels are relatively cold. The fish rise to the surface.

SUMMER

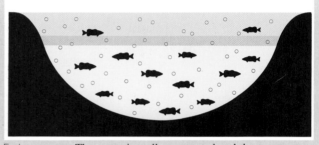

Early summer. The water is well-oxygenated and the temperature ideal for producing an abundance of food. Fish range throughout the lake to take advantage of the food supply. The predators may be anywhere. The angler cannot afford to overlook any possible lie.

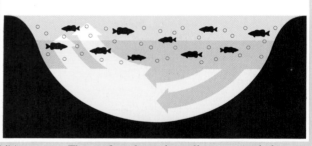

Mid-summer. The surface layer is well oxygenated, but too warm, while the waters of the hypolimnion are beginning to be low in oxygen. The fish will tend to lie in the middle depths.

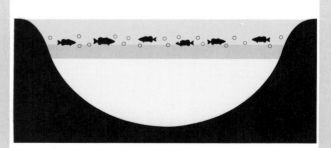

Late summer. Little change. The surface water is still too hot for most fish, and the depths are now even poorer in oxygen. The fish remain in the intermediate zones.

As well as depth, wind, current and temperature, the abundance of organic matter in the water may influence these mass movements of fish. A thinly populated body of water always retains more oxygen than one teeming with living organisms. It is therefore vital to observe the water and try to determine its quality, to mark the wind direction, pick out deep holes and trenches, and look for the weed beds where oxygen is produced.

Scientists distinguish three strata in a body of water. The surface layer, known as the epilimnion, is stirred by the wind and rich in dissolved oxygen. The middle layer is the thermocline, less rich in oxygen but more constant in temperature. Finally, in the depth of the lake, or hypolimnion, there is little change in temperature throughout the year. By the end of winter, however, the dissolved oxygen level may be running very low.

FALL

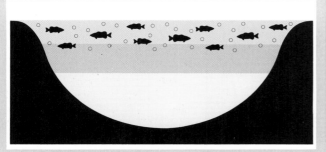

Early fall. Colder nights lower the surface temperature. The depths of the lake are warmer but still poor in oxygen. The fish rise to the surface.

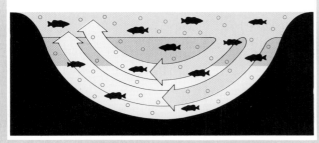

Mid-fall. As in spring, the water temperature balances out again as the wind stirs the surface and the well-oxygenated upper layers are drawn down into the depths. The lake is regenerated and the fish range everywhere.

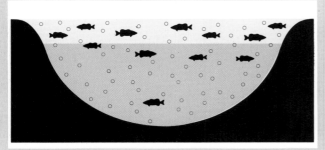

Late fall. The surface layers cool down on contact with the atmosphere, while the middle and lower depths remain warm and well oxygenated. The fish begin to sink down.

WINTER

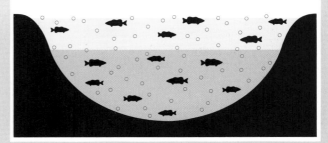

Early winter. The cold spreads downward. Ice may inhibit the interchange of gases with the atmosphere. The surface layers are coldest. The fish keep to the deepest parts of the lake.

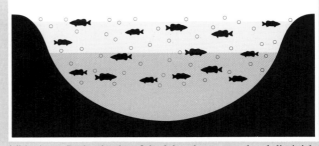

Mid-winter. In the depths of the lake, the oxygen level diminishes. Starved of oxygen, the fish rise toward the surface, where the water, though very cold, is richer in oxygen. This tendency is accentuated if the lake is iced over.

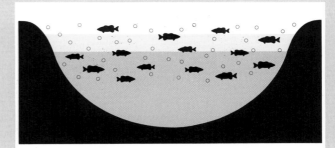

Late winter. The fish have used up all the reserves of oxygen. They crowd together near the surface, despite the bitter cold. Areas free of ice are the most favored. In frozen pools, fish may well die of asphyxiation.

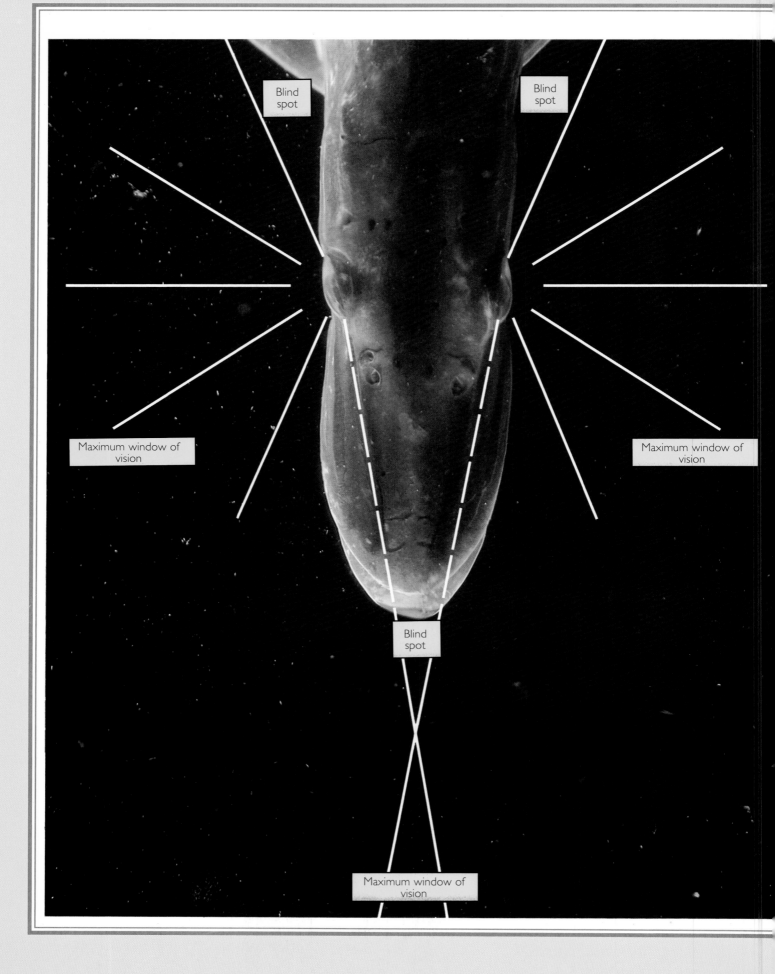

Blind spot

Blind spot

Maximum window of vision

Maximum window of vision

Blind spot

Maximum window of vision

FISH SENSES

Fish are perfectly adapted to their aquatic environment. In common with other animals, they possess the senses of sight, hearing, smell and touch. They also have a lateral line which functions like radar, enabling them to sense danger and the presence of potential prey in areas outside their field of vision.

The lateral line

The line runs along the fish's side, roughly at mid-height. It consists of tiny holes connected to nerve endings, enabling the fish to register vibrations in the water and discern the shape, speed and direction of any animal or object creating a disturbance. As a result, small fish are alerted to the presence of predators without seeing them. Similarly, pike and walleye sense the position of the shoals of roach they habitually hunt. It is by virtue of their lateral line that fish are able to navigate in even the murkiest waters.

Sight

As in the case of the human eye, the fish's retina has both rod and cone-shaped receptor cells, sensitive to the intensity of light and to color.

American studies have shown that some fish species are far sharper-sighted than others. The largemouth bass has excellent color vision. In bright sunlight, near to the surface, the bass distinguished colors more acutely than we do. Other fish, walleye or perch for instance, are less well endowed: they see in only two colors, orange and green.

Light rays are refracted and reflected by water. At deeper levels, fish perceive fewer colors than they would at the surface. Red is the first to go, then yellow and finally blue. Some fish are particularly well equipped to distinguish these colors. For this reason, red and white spoons or yellow, blue and violet plugs often give good results in deep waters. The fact that trout are very selective and will only take one sort of insect in certain light conditions may also be partly a question of color or even gradation of color.

How far a fish can see below the surface depends on the clarity of the water. Its perception of the world above and beyond its own element – its window of vision – increases the deeper it lies. Outside this window, and the reflections that fall within it, it sees nothing.

Hearing

Water is a good conductor of vibrations. These are picked up by the fish's "ears" and also, as we have noted, by the lateral line, so try not to walk heavily along the banks of rivers and lakes.

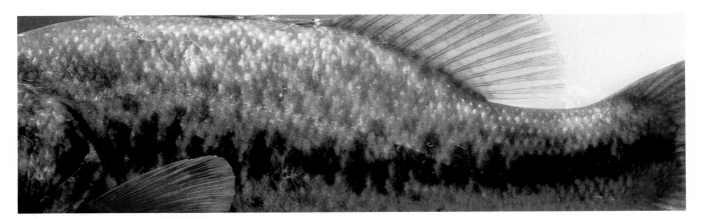

The pike's field of vision. Behind the eyes, the pike is "blind". Each eye sweeps a wide area to the side of the fish, and below. To determine the distance of an object or potential prey, the pike best perceives it with both eyes. For a predatory species, the importance of the lateral line is obvious. In addition, the sense of smell enables the pike to track its prey before having sight of it.

The lateral line is clearly visible on the flanks of the fish as a broken series of small dashes. More pronounced in some species than in others, it enables the fish to explore the vast area outside its field of vision, which explains why a fish will make good its escape, even when approached from behind. A fish easily perceives the vibrations caused by a fisherman's footsteps.

APPROACHING THE FISH

As we have seen, fish are very well equipped to detect a potential danger. The slightest movement, the flash of sunlight on a rod ring, is sufficient to alert a trout or pike, if it comes within its window of vision. It is therefore very important that the fisherman remains concealed as he changes position.

The lower a fish lies in the water, the wider its window of vision. This should be borne in mind when fishing a clear river, especially since a trout's camouflage often makes it extremely difficult to detect from the bank.

Even close to the surface, the fish's window of vision is not as limited as it might appear. A trout is never as stationary as shown in the drawing. Its movements, and the reflection of light rays, considerably increase what it is able to see of the world above the surface. The fisherman must therefore avoid standing upright on the bank. The lower his profile, the less visible he will be. He should approach stealthily, placing his feet with care, and should crouch down when crossing open ground. Avoid pointing the rod high in the air.

Take advantage of available cover when moving from one spot to another. A fisherman who remains perfectly still, even within the fish's window of vision, will give no cause for alarm.

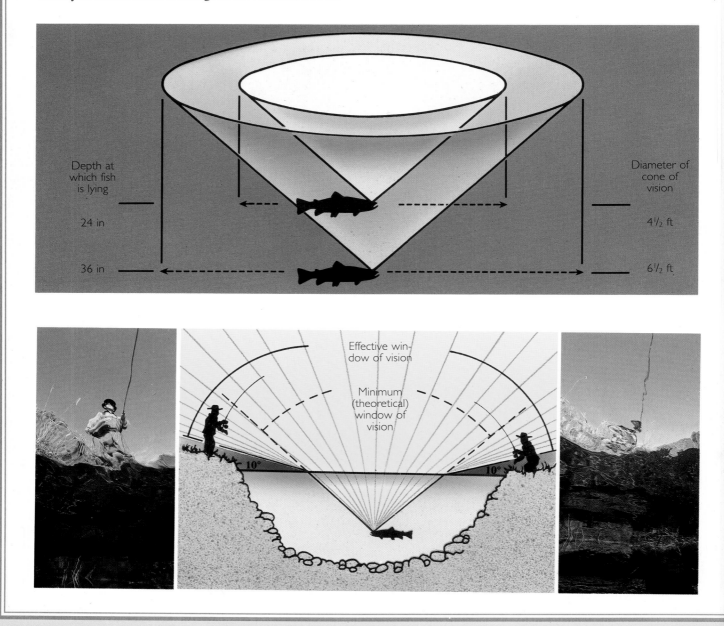

Depth at which fish is lying

24 in

36 in

Diameter of cone of vision

4½ ft

6½ ft

Effective window of vision

Minimum (theoretical) window of vision

10°

10°

HABITAT AND BEHAVIOR

The behavior of predatory fish is related to their hunting methods, which in turn depend on their environment. The trout lies on the edge of the stream, waiting for the current to deliver his prey to him. The pike lurks in ambush, motionless, camouflaged in a weed bed, waiting for a smaller fish to swim by. The largemouth bass, which often hunts at the surface, also takes advantage of weed cover to approach an unsuspecting frog. Perch and walleye hunt in packs. Wolf-like, a number of fish pursue the smaller fry and attempt an encircling maneuver, hemming them into the bank. These hunting expeditions are often spectacular, the fry shooting around on the surface trying to escape the jaws of their attackers, but at other times the predators seek shelter, in the lee of a rocky outcrop, in areas of shade. Where the law of the jungle prevails, the hunter may quickly become the hunted. To escape their predators, perch like to keep out of the sunlight, preferring places where the stripes on their flanks will blend in with the surroundings.

Predators follow the shoals of fish on which they prey, whose feeding habits and oxygen requirements are linked to seasonal water movements (see pages 14 and 15).

The only game fish which do not obey these laws are the various species of Atlantic and Pacific salmon. These marine predators return to fresh water only to breed. On the long journey to their spawning grounds – several months for the Pacific species and up to a year for the Atlantic salmon – they eat nothing. They nevertheless retain their aggressive, predatory instincts, and will snap at a lure or fly that trespasses on their space. The rivers are in spate when they reach fresh water and, after swimming and scaling rapids for several days, like trout they will rest behind rocks or in places sheltered from the current, though never in completely still water.

In open water, light is an important factor. Whereas, in winter, shoals of bait fish will seek the warmer, sun-lit layer at the surface (drawing the game fish up with them), most of the year the opposite is true. They favor the shadowy depths, where they are less visible. Predatory fish are similarly concerned to conceal themselves as much as possible.

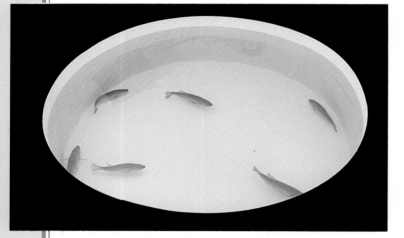

The bass have been placed in a white container, under intense light. They move about restlessly. Without a place of refuge, they feel ill at ease.

Part of the container has been covered over. The fish congregate in the shaded area, remaining almost stationary. In this way, they keep out of sight of predators and may go unnoticed.

This experiment illustrates the behavior of predatory fish, who may in turn become a prey to larger species. All species behave in exactly the same way as the young bass featured here.

In their natural environment, fish seek out a place where they will be hidden from predators while able to observe their own prey. The best swims tend to be occupied by the larger fish.

Pebbles have been substituted for the covering shelter. The fish congregate above them, fairly well camouflaged by their dark backs. They remain stationary.

A dark line has been painted on the wall of the container. The fish are drawn to it and remain in its vicinity, but the bottom of the container is brightly lit and they are restless.

A river bank with branches overhanging the surface provides an excellent swim for perch or largemouths. They wait for land-based insects and small vertebrates to fall accidentally into the water. The congregating fish may well attract a pike.

The margins of a stream and places where the river bed broadens out after rapids are good places to look for trout. In warmer waters further downstream, pike seek out similar swims. Perch are also drawn to the stiller waters on the edge of the current.

At the tail-end of a rapid, the river broadens out and the flow of water slackens. A good spot for trout and other game fish, a swim of this kind should be fished where the water begins to slow down. The margins of the current are particularly promising.

An island in mid-stream is bound to offer some excellent swims. The calm area downstream is generally occupied by walleyes. Make a careful survey of deep holes and inlets, the places where fish tend to rest or lie in wait.

Rocks in a large river provide shelter for all kinds of fish: walleyes, salmon, large trout, for example. Though productive, resting places of this kind are relatively difficult to fish without a boat, being so far out from the bank.

Trout do not always hunt at the surface. This one is investigating a weed bed, where larvae and small fry are to be had. Trout are not averse to strong currents. They tend to watch over a large area, where no drifting prey escapes them.

Piles of wood always offer opportunities to the game fisherman. In the middle reaches of a river, largemouths, walleyes, perch and pike will often use them for cover. You risk losing hooks and traces, but it is worth it if you end up hooking a big fish.

Rapids always mean good fishing, for trout and other species. Trout tend to take up a station on the slacker margins of the white water. In the middle reaches of a river, such swims will also attract other predators.

SWIMS IN FAST-FLOWING RIVERS

In fast-flowing rivers, most fish take up station on the edge of the current, where they can watch over a large area while conserving energy. This considerably limits the areas over which the fisherman need cast his spinner or bait, provided he can discern the spots where a fish is likely to lie. Fish have little time to examine the prey brought to them on the current and, as long as nothing is done to alarm them, will readily take the bait.

The flow of most rivers is irregular. The current speeds up and slows down as it encounters shallows and submerged rocks. Once practiced in observing different configurations, the fisherman will be able to identify likely hunting grounds.

The best swims are always occupied by the biggest fish. Competition between predators inevitably relegates the weaker to the least favorable spots. A fisherman who only ever catches small specimens needs to improve his methods of prospecting.

Trout will usually hug the bank, where they can keep watch over a large area of the main stream while remaining out of sight. At the slightest disturbance, they take refuge under the overhang carved out by the current.

A surface eddy in an area of otherwise smooth water indicates a submerged obstacle, an ideal lie for a trout in cold water, for a group of perch or a pike in warmer rivers. The fish are likely to station themselves on the margins of the currents which flow round the obstacle.

The piles of a bridge offer excellent cover for all species of predatory fish. They tend to lie downstream, on the edge of the still water, sometimes at a considerable distance from the obstruction. In trout rivers it is also worth prospecting above the bridge: a fish may be lurking against the pile itself.

A fallen tree trunk is always a good place to look for trout. The principle is the same as with other obstacles: the fish keeps in the shadow, where it is least visible and yet can look out over a large area. If an item of prey swims past, the trout darts out to catch it, then retires into cover until the next sortie.

A rock projecting above the water is an opportunity not to be missed. The fish may lie behind it, where the divided flow of water reunites, to one side or upstream of the obstacle or, if the river is in flood, in the calm water in its lee. The latter is the most likely spot in springtime.

REPRODUCTION

Not all predatory species reproduce in the same way or at the same time of year. The perch family and pike spawn in early spring, when the water is beginning to warm up; salmon lay their eggs in the fall, or even in the depths of winter, when the rivers are at their coldest.

The pike

The pike is similar in its habits to members of the perch family. At the end of winter, the females, usually much larger in size than the males, seek out shallow coves, river banks and submerged water meadows and reed beds. It takes several males to fertilize the eggs of one female. The fertilized eggs are attached to a solid object, where they incubate for several days. The alevin which eventually emerges has a sucker-like mouth, with which to hold on to water weed. Once the yolk sac has been completely absorbed, the young fish begins feeding on zooplankton, then tiny invertebrates. By six weeks old (generally, in early May), the young pike, or jack, is fully formed and becomes a fish-eater, quickly developing a territorial instinct.

Perch, bass and walleyes

The perch lays strings of eggs on submerged branches and water weed. The walleyes and bass keep a constant watch over their "nest", waving their pectoral fins to ensure a supply of oxygen to the eggs.

The salmon family

Trout and salmon reproduce in cold, fast-running rivers. The water temperature needs to be between 39 and 43°F.

Of all fish, salmon undertake the longest, most arduous journeys in order to reproduce. The Pacific salmon breeds only once in its life. It leaves the ocean to reach its breeding grounds and, once it has spawned, dies, exhausted, in the space of a few days.

Most of the salmon tribe require cold running water with a high oxygen content. Some lake-dwelling species, such as the cristivomer (Canadian lake trout) or the sockeye salmon spawn in situ.

As the breeding season (fall or winter) approaches, the males undergo considerable changes. Their jaws become elongated and hooked, and some species develop larger, more powerful teeth, with which to fight off rivals. The changes in coloration are most striking: male Pacific salmon are silvery when they leave the Pacific but become completely red as they ascend the rivers.

Spawning takes place over beds of gravel. Several males may attend a single female, the largest driving off the others. The female digs out a hollow with her tail, then approaches the male, rubbing herself against him to get him to fertilize her eggs. The two fish soon begin to

The bass is the predator with the most complex behavior pattern. The female lays her eggs in a nest on the bottom. The male watches over the brood and defends them against predators, whatever their size (he has no hesitation in attacking a human intruder!). During the incubation period, he fans the eggs with his large pectoral fins to provide a good supply of oxygen. When the young emerge, the male bass redoubles his efforts, abandoning his progeny to their fate only when the yolk sac has been completely absorbed and the young fish are able to fend for themselves.

quiver and shake. They then stiffen, arch their backs and, mouths open wide, together release their eggs and milt into the hollow. The female covers the eggs with coarse gravel as a protection from the many predators – trout and other salmon – which would otherwise make a good meal of them.

This behavior is repeated several times, the couple moving some distance away and digging a new hollow each time. When many fish are active over the spawning ground, new arrivals tend to destroy the nests already made. The eggs are carried away by the current, making a feast for opportunist young trout.

This exceptional photograph shows two char just prior to the act of releasing their milt and eggs. The couples which form at spawning time generally remain together throughout the season. But this is not always so. It would appear that with certain species, the brown trout being a case in point, there is an excess of females over males.

The males are therefore obliged to fertilize the eggs of several females.

After spawning, freshwater members of the salmon family do not die as do some species of the salmon but, being exhausted, lie low in the vicinity of the spawning grounds until the spring floods. The current then carries them back the way they came with such effort some months before.

The fertilized ova remain under the gravel for some months, usually hatching out in the spring. Weighed down by their heavy yolk sacs, the alevins tend to stay put until they are able to swim. They then emerge from hiding and swim to the surface, beginning their adult life with all its attendant dangers.

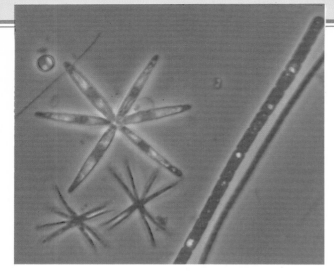

Phytoplankton. By photosynthesis, they fix various mineral elements and manufacture proteins. For this to take place, there must be adequate heat and light. Without phytoplankton, aquatic life would be impossible.

WHAT FISH EAT

Pure water is devoid of life. For living organisms to develop, they must absorb mineral salts, particularly nitrogenous matter, which are the nutrients of phytoplankton, the first stage in the food chain. By the process of photosynthesis, phytoplankton transform mineral into organic matter. The phytoplankton in turn support zooplankton, and so on up the food chain, from multicellular crustaceans to insects and fish. Predatory fish exist at the apex of this pyramid, feeding variously on fish, insects and the larger crustaceans.

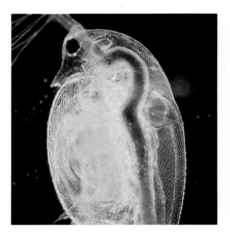

Zooplankton. Organisms of this kind form the diet of small fish, which are in turn devoured by predators. The food chain can only work if there is a balance between each successive link.

Each link in the food chain preys on the preceding link and is preyed on by the next link up. Only the very biggest fish are not subject to this law.

Fish are all more or less predatory. Some, like the perch, specialize in capturing small fry. The pike prefers to get its teeth into some of its bigger neighbors.

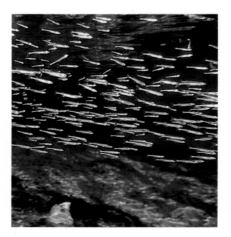

Plankton also make up the diet of the aquatic insects which spend much of their life cycle under water. The winged, adult stage of their life may be just long enough for them to breed.

The fry of fish emerge in vast quantities each spring. They transform plankton into an appetizing meal for bigger predators.

The wind plays a part in food distribution. A windward shore is generally richer in plankton, in turn attracting all the other links in the food chain.

Of all the freshwater predators the pike is the most voracious. It feeds mainly on cyprinids, but will not refuse fellow predators, even if they have a few spines, like the perch, the walleye or the catfish – or the pike.

Some fish nevertheless escape the maw of this rapacious feeder. Bream and carp of more than 2 lb in weight are too deep in the body for the pike to swallow. They may however get a severe mauling.

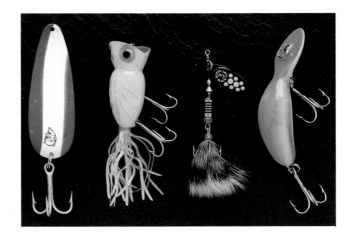

Fishermen could restrict themselves to livebaits in angling for game fish. Some think it more sporting to use lures, simulating the movement of fish and other food in the water. Flexible plastics have made it possible to manufacture highly effective imita-

tions of frogs and worms. Plugs are made of wood or plastic and, thanks to their diving vane, can be made to rise and fall in the water, like a real fish. Spoons imitate a swimming fish, while spinners give off vibrations which attract predators.

HOOKS

The hook is the least expensive item in a fisherman's tackle box, yet the most important. There are many different types, and several factors have to be considered in choosing the right one for a given situation.

Over the last few years, eyed hooks have tended to replace the spade-end variety. The game fisherman should choose the eyed type, even when fishing for perch with insect baits, because it can be tied far more securely.

Shape is extremely important. There are hooks with long shanks, short shanks, curved points, and so on. Watch out for defects. The hook should be properly finished. Test the point to ensure that it is sharp. The configuration of the barb should also be taken into account: for fish with a hard mouth, such as pike, too angled a barb may hinder penetration on the strike and be the cause of many lost fish. Microbarbs are more than adequate for most fish, and barbless hooks are widely used in Britain.

The thickness of the shank also varies. Fine-wire hooks are often chosen to keep weight down, but more robust ones are needed for dealing with big fish.

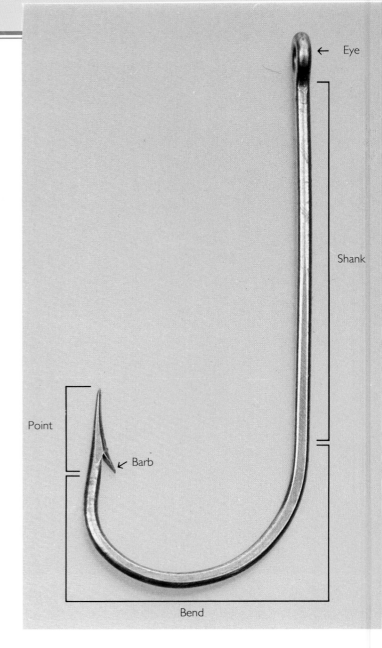

Hooks come in all shapes and sizes. The ones shown here are all eyed hooks, of the kind used by American and British fishermen. New carp-fishing techniques have made European anglers aware of their advantages. If the eye is well formed, the line will not be harmed by sharp edges, as is the case with spade-end hooks. Spade-end hooks are more practical when fishing for really small fish. This is rarely the case with game fishermen, except when they are wanting to catch bait fish.

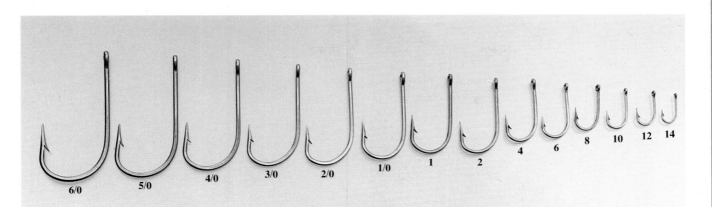

Hooks are manufactured in a range of sizes. The higher the number, the smaller the hook. As each shape of hook is designed for a certain kind of fishing, the range of sizes is in fact limited: there would be no point in producing fine-wire hooks for catching roach with a worm bait in the larger sizes. Conversely, there would be no use for small versions of heavy-gauge salmon hooks. All manufacturers use the same numbering system, but do not imagine that all n°14 hooks are identical! There can be quite significant differences.

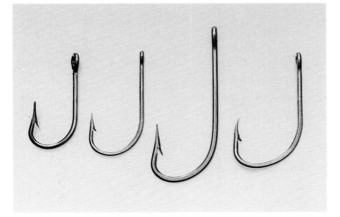

The length of the shank is an important factor. If you are going to bait the hook with a dead fish, the shank needs to be fairly long. However, experience teaches that fish tend to get off a hook with a long shank more easily and, wherever possible, hooks with medium or short shanks are to be preferred.

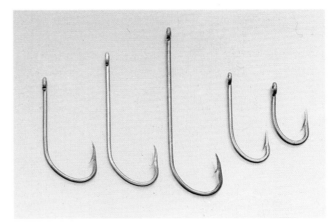

The thickness of the wire will depend on the size of your quarry. Roach, bleak and small fish generally are prone to be hook shy (a fine-wire type is therefore indicated); the larger species may crush or straighten a hook that is not strong enough.

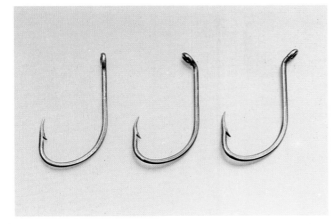

The position of the eye is another factor to consider. A straight configuration is best with natural baits. Hooks with the eye angled up or down are often considered more suitable for making artificial flies: the former for dry, the latter for wet flies.

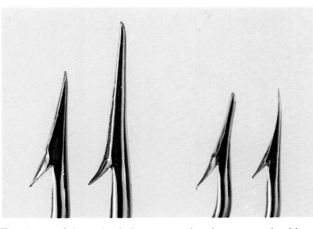

The shape of the point is important when it comes to hooking your fish. With a short point, the barb penetrates rapidly, but tends to work free more easily. A long point calls for a firmer strike. A sharp point, designed to facilitate penetration of the barb, is obviously best in almost every case.

LOOKING AFTER YOUR HOOKS

Most fisherman neglect to check that their hooks are sharp before beginning a day's sport. This is a mistake, since even top-quality hooks can be blunted or broken by obstacles on the bottom. Many good fish are lost in this way. Depending on the way they have been stored, even new hooks can be defective.

Make a firm resolution. Every time you go fishing or change your bait, check the condition of the point of the hook. Fishermen often fail to change the treble hooks of lures, spoons or plugs simply because it takes time.

Nor is it always necessary to change the hook. If the point is damaged, it can often be restored by sharpening.

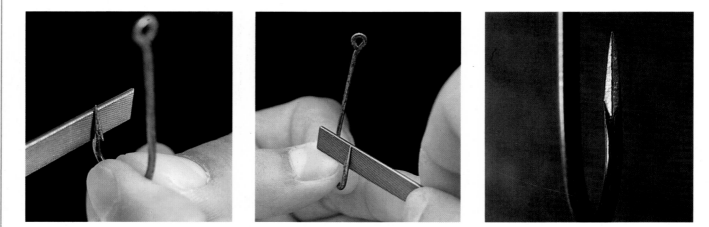

Restoring the point of a hook with a small file is possible with larger hooks. It is a valuable technique with the hooks on a lure, which tend to be difficult to change. Otherwise, it is preferable to select a new hook, ensuring that it is properly finished.

Sharpening with a stone, on the other hand, is vital if you are to keep your hooks in perfect condition. A stone of this kind – or a modern, specially produced diamond file, suitable also for small hooks – is essential for keeping hooks in good order.

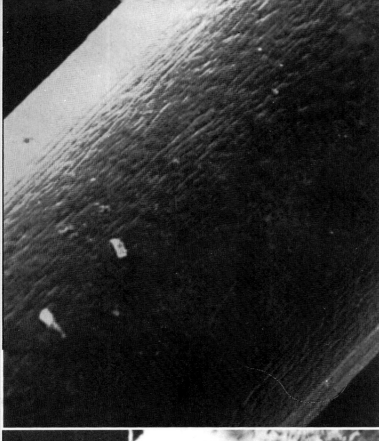

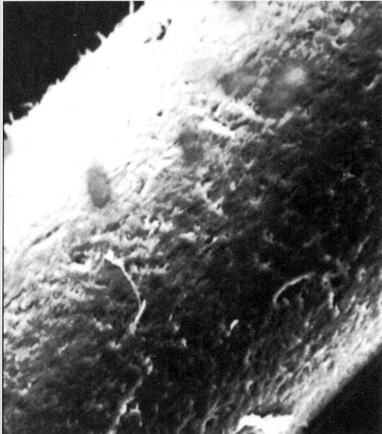

Nylon wears, as a result of rubbing against the linings of the rod rings. Examination under the microscope reveals tiny scratches on the surface of the line.

Light is another enemy of fishing lines. They should be stored in the dark, and extremes of temperature should be avoided.

LINES

The advent of synthetic materials was of great benefit to all fishermen. A wide range of strong, flexible lines are now available, and they are improving all the time.

Monofilament lines are the most widely used. Thanks to modern manufacturing techniques, they can be extremely fine and reliable, and are now being produced for specific purposes. Fishermen who cast long distances need a line which "shoots" well without stretch if they are to strike and hook their fish effectively. Anglers using natural baits, on the other hand, must use a supple, fairly elastic line if it is not to break on the strike. The anglers maneuvering a deadbait will be looking for a highly visible, fluorescent line, so that they can observe its behavior and detect the slightest take.

Pike lines

There has been considerable progress in this field in recent years. The pike is endowed with wicked teeth which will make short work of nylon, so the trace must be of a material which will not shear. Steel traces are still used, but they lack flexibility. The latest products are made of Kevlar or nylon, with a steel core, the latter being essential for strength.

Fly-fishing lines

An artificial fly is too light to be cast like a spoon. The technique therefore calls for a heavy, whip-like line to carry the fly to the fish. The leader linking flyline to fly is made of nylon but, to ensure that the fly lands delicately on the water, normally tapers toward the fly. Manufacturers produce one-piece nylon leaders, but some anglers prefer to make their own by joining progressively finer lengths of nylon.

KNOTS

Knots are a necessary evil; points of weakness, where a breakage is most likely to occur. Of the many that exist, some are better than others, tending not to crush the nylon. Each time the nylon is pinched, it flattens and the strain is concentrated on only a part of its diameter, eventually causing it to rupture and shear.

Tying a good knot is therefore an indispensable skill. Only two are absolutely essential: one for tying a hook; one for joining two lengths of nylon together. To help in forming an even knot, moisten the ends of nylon to lubricate before drawing them tight.

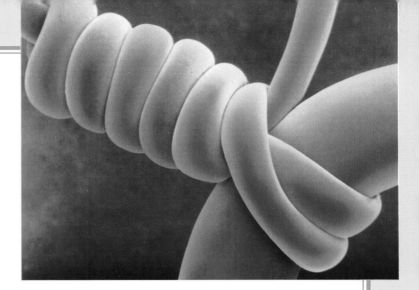

This knot attaching hook to line is a good strong one. The pressure is evenly distributed over each turn in the nylon and the two bends around the eye of the hook are not drawn so tight as to cause a break. It has one fault, though: it has a tendency to slip.

When nylon is drawn too tight, it tends to break where the distortion is greatest. The weakness may not be visible to the naked eye, but it is where the break will eventually occur. The danger can be avoided by tying good knots and retying them at regular intervals.

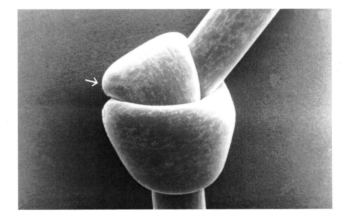

How a knot weakens the nylon is evident from this picture. The line will rupture at the point of greatest distortion. Always make sure that there are no knots of this type in your line: a breakage is inevitable.

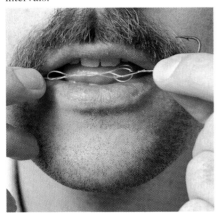

Moistening the line before drawing a knot tight lessens friction and ensures the best possible distribution of pressure. This minimizes the weakness in the line represented by the knot.

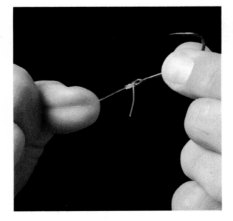

Draw the knot tight gradually, then pull hard to ensure that it is properly formed. Better to have the line break at this point than when you are fighting a fine fish.

Having tested the knot, trim off the loose end, taking care not to nick the line itself. This is another frequent cause of breaking.

KNOTS THAT ALL FISHERMEN SHOULD KNOW

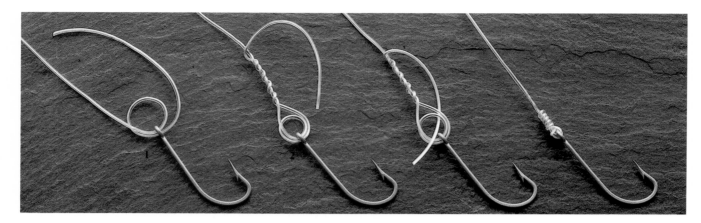

Clinch knot. Strength 90%. Pass the end twice through the eye of the hook (1). Turn it four or five times round the line (2). Bring it back through the two loops in the eye (3). Pull tight (4). Using nail-clippers, trim the end close to the knot so that it will not cause any unwanted disturbance in the water. This is one of the strongest knots in the business and is ideal for attaching artificial flies.

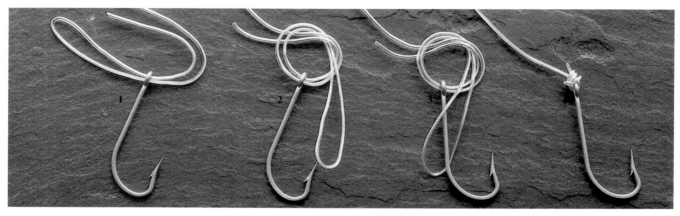

The Palomar knot. Strength 85%. Pass doubled end of line through the eye of the hook (1). Tie overhand knot in doubled line (2). Pull the looped end over the hook (3). Pull tight and trim the unwanted end (4). The advantage of this knot is that the hook is held firmly as an extension to the line. It is suitable for attaching artificial flies and lures.

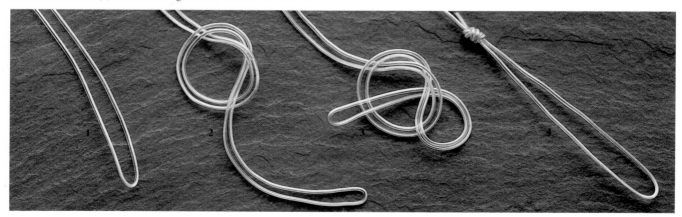

Forming a loop. Strength 70%. Double the end back along the line (1). Tie an overhand knot (2). Pass the looped end back through the knot (3). Draw tight to form loop (4). This is useful for joining a leader to the reel line or for attaching a lure, which needs freedom to travel through the water realistically. Joining loop to loop is a quick and easy matter, but it does detract somewhat from the strength of the line.

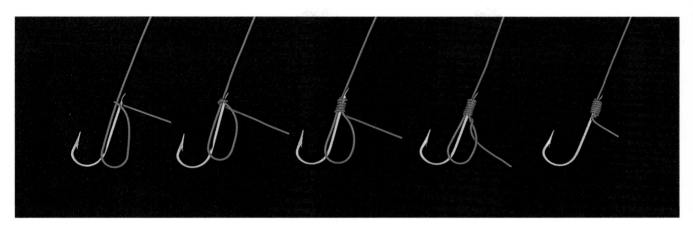

Spade end whip. Strength 80%. Double the end of the line along-side the hook (1). Loop the free end round hook and line and make five or six turns (2). Pass the free end through doubled line (3). Pull on both parts of the line, making sure that knot tightens evenly and that the turns round the hook do not override one another (4 and 5). There are other possible knots, but this is the least complicated.

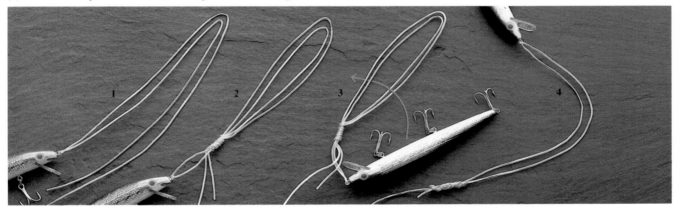

Attaching a plug (artificial fish). Strength 76%. Pass free end through the eye of the plug (1). Form a large loop and make three turns around the doubled line just above the plug (2). Pass the plug through the large double loop (3). Pull tight (4). This method is particularly suitable for plugs with a diving vane, which will work less effectively if obstructed. The angle of the diving vane controls the movement of the lure.

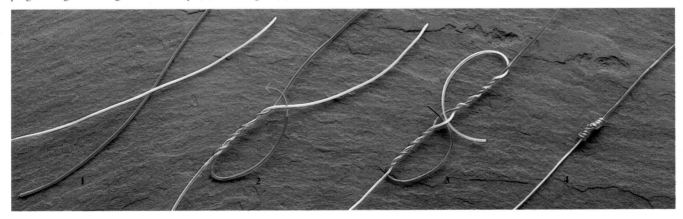

Joining two lengths of nylon: the blood knot. Strength 65%. Overlap the ends of the two lines, laying one across the other (1). Take one end and wind it round the opposing line, then bring it back through the first loop (2). Hold it in this position and repeat the process with the free end of the other line (3). Pull tight (4). The advantage of this knot is that the two connected lengths form a straight line.

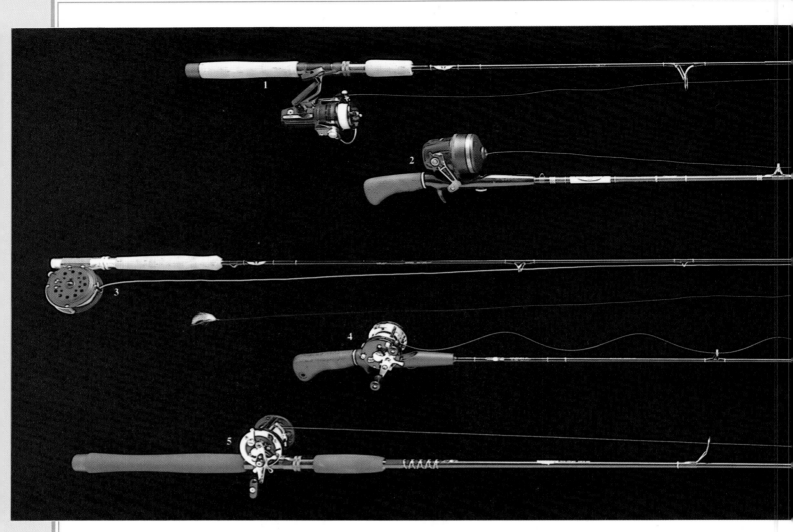

RODS AND REELS

Predatory fish patrol large areas, often far from the bank. They can be caught at rod's length. Since it may be necessary to retrieve a lure or deadbait rapidly through the water, the requirements are a long rod and tackle that can be cast a long way and retrieved rapidly, perhaps on occasion imparting irregular movements to the bait in imitation of a prey fish.

Modern casting rods are made of carbon fiber or boron, light yet powerful enough for casting long distances. For artificial lures, an 8ft rod is quite adequate; but for casting and retrieving a deadbait, a rod of up to 12ft is more suitable. This makes for a wider angle between line and bottom, ensuring that the dead fish travels smoothly through the water without snagging stones and other obstacles.

For boat-fishing a shorter rod is appropriate (8ft), as the fisherman can get close to his quarry and is generally working the bait through deeper water.

A fixed-spool reel is the type most commonly used. Select one with a fairly high gearing ratio for rapid retrieval. There is a vast number of models to choose from. Anglers tend to go for a reel bigger than they really need. All freshwater fish can be caught using a medium-sized reel, which has the advantage of lightness. Quality, on the other hand, is of paramount importance. The drag mechanism should be adjustable, giving out line when the fish makes a run. The gearing mechanism can easily be put under great strain by a powerful fish such as the salmon. It is therefore wise to choose a top-of-the-range model, which will last longer, and is not likely to let you

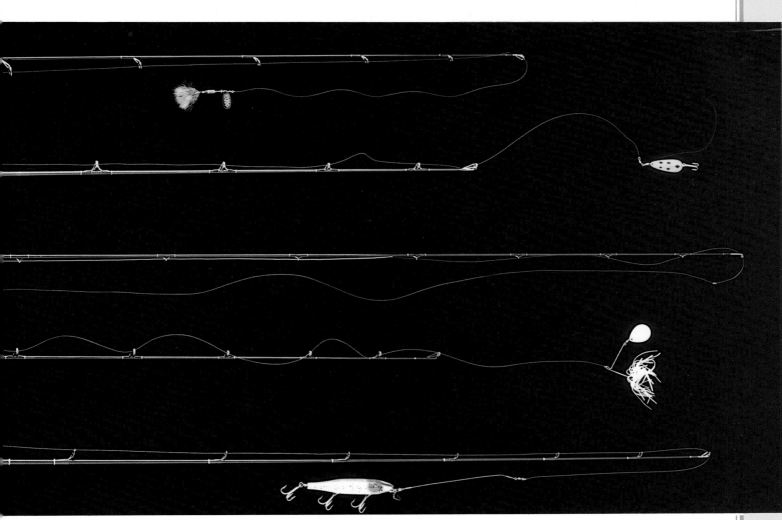

(1) Bait-casting rod with fixed-spool reel. The guide rings are on the underside of the rod.
(2) American-style casting rod: the rings are on the upper side.(3) Fly-fishing rod with manual, center-pin reel. (4 and 5) Bait-casting rods with multiplier-type reels. NOTE All except the fly reel are shown mounted for left handed anglers.

down when playing a fine fighting fish.

Unlike American fishermen, Europeans make less use of multiplier reels. A few anglers have begun to appreciate their qualities, and they may well have a bright future over here. They offer many advantages: an experienced fisherman can cast just as far as with a fixed-spool reel, and contact with the fish is more direct. They are generally of high quality, and have a progressive checking mechanism. They are especially suitable for such strong fighters as salmon.

To cast a heavy lure, all the fisherman needs do is free the line and rely on the action of the rod. In fly-fishing the technique is just the opposite. As the lure is extremely light, the fly is carried to its destination by the weight of the line. This heavy, tapered line, formerly made of silk, is propelled by a special rod, whippier in action than the kind of rod used for bait-casting. For trout, relatively short rods are used: 6–9 ft for river fishing, 10 ft for lakes. For salmon, a two-handed rod 13–15 ft in length is preferred. The reel serves simply to hold the line and backing in reserve. It may be manual or automatic (with a retrieve mechanism actuated by a lever).

Fly fishing is currently winning many new adherents. Though the technique was originally developed for trout and salmon, it is now used to catch all kinds of fresh- and saltwater predators. It makes for better sport: a fish hooked on a fly puts up a far stronger fight.

CHOOSING A SUITABLE ROD

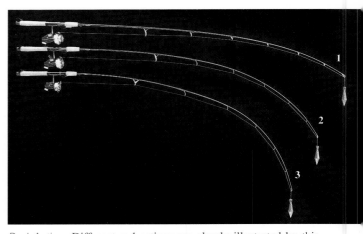

Rod Action. Different rod actions are clearly illustrated by this experiment. Note how the three rods bend with an identical weight attached to the end. The first rod has a tip action; the second is of medium stiffness, flexing to half its length; the third is said to have a through action.

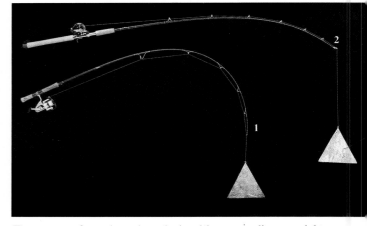

The power of a rod can be calculated by suspending a weight from the tip, until the tip is tangential to the vertical. Rod nº 2 has the rod rings on the upper side, in the American style. A powerful rod of this kind is suitable for taking both sea fish and freshwater predators.

There is a practically unlimited choice of rods, and selecting the one best suited to a particular kind of fishing can be a perplexing task.

The action of a rod is determined by its degree of taper, the size of its constituent parts and the material of which it is made. It is easy to confuse the action and the power of a rod, but they are not the same thing. Action describes the way in which a rod works: whether it flexes throughout its length (through action) or mainly in its upper section (tip action); power is a measure of the weight it can cast.

Sensitivity describes the rod's aptitude to transmit vibrations on the line, the tug of a fish, or even the bumping of a lure over the bottom. When deadbaiting with a moving bait, sensitivity of this kind is extremely important, making it possible to discern the behavior of the dead fish and impart to it the movements most appropriate to the quarry. A pike, say, is not lured in the same way as a walleye.

All rods are now made of composite materials. Despite its sensitivity, fiberglass has been virtually abandoned as being too heavy and "floppy" in favor of carbon fiber, which is stronger and more rigid. Boron rods are very light and moderately sensitive.

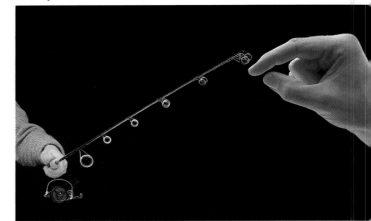

A rod's sensitivity can be tested by striking the top ring with the finger. If the rod is sensitive, the vibrations will be felt in the handle. The number of rings and their position are also important factors.

Tip action is suitable for lure fishing from the bank and whenever a heavy concentrated weight needs to be cast.

Through action is appropriate for fly fishing, and use of baits with float tackle.

In the United States and the UK, it is common to use fairly soft-action rods for playing quite big fish.

Rods for casting light and ultra-light tackle have a soft action. The rod rings are on the underside and, on casting, the line touches the intermediate sections of rod.

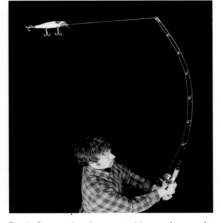

Rods for casting heavy tackle, such as saltwater rods, have the rod rings uppermost when a multiplier is in use. In France, they are now used for freshwater fishing and are likely to become increasingly popular.

When fishing for large pike in areas with many obstructions, a rigid rod is required to head the fish off from underwater obstacles, which the pike may exploit to break free.

Three rod sections, identical in strength but with different diameters. The boron rod (right) is the most sensitive. The carbon fiber (middle) is stiffer and less sensitive. The section (left) is made of fiberglass.

Metal sleeves and ferrules for joining the sections of a rod decrease its sensitivity and are no longer used on top-quality rods. Carbon-fiber or boron spigot joints have far less effect on the action of the rod.

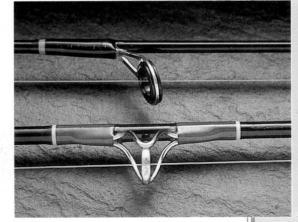

Rod rings may have one, two or three legs. Single-leg rings are very sensitive, but also more fragile. Those with two legs are stronger but may tend to impair the action of a light, bendy rod.

NATURAL BAITS

All game fish can be caught on natural baits. Worms and aquatic insects form the main diet of trout and perch. Pike and walleyes feed on other fish.

Knowledge of aquatic insects is therefore of prime importance for the trout fisherman. He must be able to distinguish the main orders of insect, imitate them if he intends to use artificial flies, and capture them if he wants to offer them as livebait.

The best-known aquatic insect is the mayfly, a member of the Order Ephemeroptera, which may live as long as two years underwater, as a larva, before attaining its adult, winged form. It then mates, lays its eggs and dies in the space of a few hours. The larva – known as nymph – makes an excellent bait.

In addition to the Ephemeroptera, our rivers are home to many other insects of the Trichoptera and Plecoptera orders (caddis flies and stoneflies), which in the adult stage fold their wings rooflike over their bodies. To protect their soft body parts, the nymphs of caddis flies form a sheath-like tube of small pieces of vegetation, grit and so on. The photograph on the facing page shows a number of caddis nymphs in their protective cases. They make excellent bait.

The life cycle of the mayfly begins with the male and female insects mating in flight (1). The female then lays her eggs on the water (2). They fall to the bottom and incubate for several days. The tiny nymphs (3) which emerge bury themselves in the sand, where they feed on decaying organic material. Their life in the water may continue for up to two years (4). The big, two-year-old nymphs are the most suitable as bait. In late spring, they leave their place of shelter and swim to the surface (5). This is the most dangerous time for them, as they are actively hunted by fish. The nymph lies in the surface film and splits open to release an immature winged insect, the subimago (a "dun" in angler's parlance). In this intermediate stage, the insect hides in the vegetation, where it undergoes another molt to become a full-blown imago (or "spinner") (7). The adult insect lives only a few hours, just time to mate and lay its eggs.

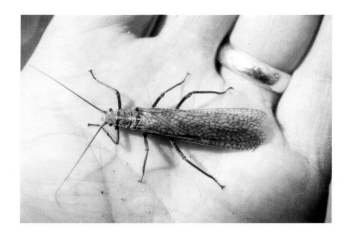

The stonefly larva, or "creeper", is a sturdy little creature, about 1 inch in length, depending on age. It hides under rocks in fast, cold streams. It lives for between three months and three years in its aquatic stage, depending on species and environment.

The adult stonefly is a large insect, easily recognizable by its slim, flat, folded wings. It is mainly of interest to big fish, big trout and sometimes salmon. Some artificial flies can simulate its appearance very effectively.

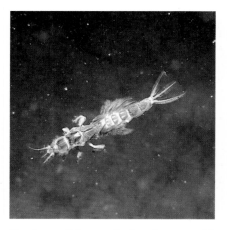

The larva of the mayfly has the powerful legs of a burrowing insect. It comes in two sizes: the two-year-old form, which will be making the transition to adult within a few weeks, and the one-year-olds, which will remain in the water for another year.

The subimago of the mayfly ("dun") has a further molt to undergo before becoming a full-blown adult. There are two species of large Ephemeroptera, which are hard to tell apart, but trout make no distinction, so fishermen need not either.

The female mayfly is bigger than the male. When they hatch out en masse, fish gorge themselves on the insects as they lay their eggs and die on the surface of the water. This is the time to catch big trout, while they are feeding with abandon.

Caddis fly or "sedge" larvae construct a protective casing. The species are legion and only a specialist can identify them all. Any of them can be used as bait for trout and perch.

The larvae can be removed from its casing before being threaded onto the hook, but it is very fragile. A better plan is to leave a part of the casing and pass the hook through that.

The cranefly larva, or leatherjacket, can be found in decaying vegetable matter. It has a segmented body. It is a useful bait for perch and large trout, and pike will sometimes condescend to take it.

The adult cranefly, resembles an overgrown mosquito. It is not a very useful natural bait, being too fragile to fix onto the hook. But used in the form of an artificial fly it can be deadly.

The dobsonfly larva *(Corydalis cornutus)*, a close cousin of the alderfly, lives in fast-flowing American rivers. It preys on young fish and other aquatic larvae. Its strong jaws can give the angler a painful nip.

The adult dobsonfly is a large, black-bodied insect with transparent wings. In the United States, it is much sought after as bait. There is no equivalent European species, the alderfly being considerably smaller in size.

Dragonfly larvae (darter shown above, the more delicate damselfly below) are formidable predators, that feed on other larvae and young fish. They live under stones, seeking shelter from the current. There are several species, of different sizes.

Adult dragonflies are especially attractive to freshwater bass, which will rise to take them. As they are difficult to capture, anglers simulate them with big artificial flies. Other fish species show little or no interest.

TROUT BAITS

Trout feed largely on aquatic insects. All the larvae illustrated on the previous pages can be used as bait.

Early spring is the time the fish will be looking for them, when the larvae abandon their cover and venture forth to become adult insects. They are then the trout's only source of food, as terrestrial insects such as grasshoppers and crickets have not yet emerged, and flood-borne worms are scarcer.

Catching the larvae is not difficult. Caddis-fly nymphs can be found by looking under stones in a stream of clear water; mayfly larvae lie buried in the organic matter on the bed. The best way is to sift through a shovelful of sand.

The adult insects can also be used, but many of them are too fragile. Only the mayfly and the larger stonefly are really suitable. As they are difficult to catch in any number, fishermen generally prefer to imitate them with artificial flies, which the fish take readily. When many different insects are drifting on the surface, trout may become choosy and take only one species. The trick is then to find the right artificial fly, the one which, by its silhouette, best simulates the trout's preference.

All types of grasshopper are suitable bait for trout. They live in large numbers along river banks and frequently fall into the water. Try fishing swims close to the bank, where long grass overhangs the stream. When fishing with a live insect, pass the hook through the skin of the thorax, as shown on the left.

Dragonfly larvae are relatively large and will attract the bigger fish. To avoid killing the creature, thread the hook through the thorax, just behind the head. Use a fairly light n°8 or n°10 hook, so as not to inhibit the movements of the larva, which are highly attractive to fish.

In America, fishermen sing the praises of the dobsonfly larva, which they present on a n°6 hook. These big larvae must be offered alive. Hold them just behind the head to avoid a bite from the strong jaws.

Adult mayfly can be used at the moment they emerge as adults. The problem is to catch sufficient for a day's fishing and keep them alive. Their larvae make a first-class bait.

The stonefly is a big insect and can be used when it emerges as an adult. Use a n°10 hook and thread it just behind the head. However, the larva is much easier to catch than the adult stonefly!

The cranefly larva can be used on a n°8 or n°10 hook, threaded just behind the head. A fragile bait, the skin easily loses its contents, so a fine, sharp hook is needed.

Caddis-fly larvae make excellent trout bait. Being very fragile, they need to be drawn slowly from their casing and fixed on a sharp, top-quality hook.

Nymphs of all kinds come into their own in the spring. Use a n°10 hook, threaded just behind the head. Some fishermen bait the hook with several larvae.

FISH EGGS

During the breeding season, members of the salmon family arrive over their spawning grounds in successive waves. The eggs laid by the first arrivals are frequently uncovered by newcomers and carried away on the current. The fish quickly get into the habit of feeding on them, and they have proved to be one of the most effective baits of all.

British and European regulations prohibit the use of fish eggs as bait, so there is no question of catching trout and salmon in this manner over there. However, more and more fishermen are going to Alaska each summer, where the practice is officially sanctioned.

The technique involves taking a small handful of the eggs and wrapping them in muslin to form a small package. This is attached to the hook and allowed to roll along the bottom with the current.

It is a sure way of catching Pacific salmon en route for their spawning grounds. The reason is not clear, since the fish do not normally feed. Snapping at a lure out of sheer aggression is understandable, but why do they go for a lifeless bait of this kind? One thing we do know is that most of the fish taken are males.

LIVEBAIT

Not all game fish enjoy the same diet. Perch and trout, as we have seen, are insect eaters; only big specimens feed on other fish. The largemouth and smallmouth bass are similar in their habits, though the predatory instinct of these voracious feeders is undoubtedly stronger. The diet of walleyes and pike consists chiefly of fish: pike tend to lie in wait for their prey; walleyes hunt in packs. Perch also hunt in this way when feeding on small fry.

European regulations forbid the use as live or deadbait of any fish species with a prescribed minimum capture weight. This immediately excludes trout, salmon, pike and zander. Perch fishing, on the other hand, is not regulated in this way, and a small perch makes an excellent livebait, tenacious of life and much appreciated by pike.

What other fish are suitable? The bass is the chief predator of the catfish, and Americans often make capital of this fact. In Europe, specialized ways of catching black bass have not been developed, as the fish are still too few in number.

For trout and perch, minnows and small gudgeon make the best livebaits, but small roach, dace and bleak are also useful. These fish have silvery sides and will attract predators from some distance, but it is advisable to use them only in waters where they occur naturally. In the UK it is illegal to transfer species of bait from one water to another.

For pike and walleyes, roach of about 3–6 inches, small tench, and chub are excellent. Some claim that the goldfish makes the best pike bait. The case is unproven. The goldfish has one advantage: like a small carp, it will survive on the hook for a long time.

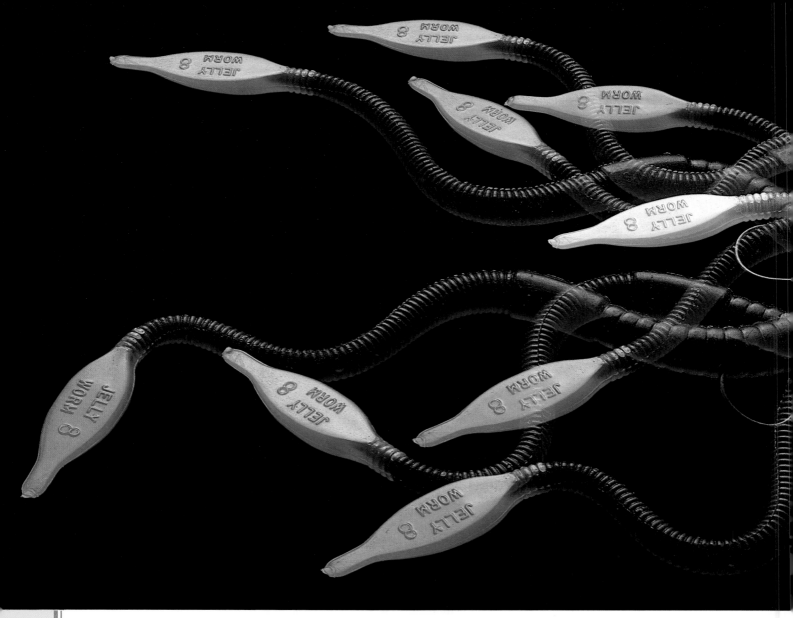

LURES

Game fish are hunters. The idea of replacing real prey by lures, which the fisherman causes to move through the water like a wounded fish, is nothing new. It is the invention of the fixed-spool reel, facilitating the casting and recovery of the lure, which has led to the immense popularity of this technique.

There are at least four basic types of lure. Metal spoons are relatively heavy. Of no particular shape, they are designed to spin or wobble through the water, and it is the vibrations and flash that provoke a reaction in fish. Artificial flies are lures made of fur and feather. Very light in weight, they are designed to simulate a larva or an insect. Streamers are bigger flies, though not based on any particular insect, often representing small fish,

leeches and so on. All predatory fish will take a fly, even pike. Plugs are made of wood or plastic. They are roughly fish-shaped and may perfectly emulate the colors and scales of certain fish species. A diving vane at the front, sometimes adjustable, causes them to rise and dive as they move through the water. They are excellent for trolling. Finally, there are flexible lures made of soft plastic. Though not usually modeled on any living creature, they are designed to move in a seductive way.

Flexible lures are especially popular in the United States. They first reached Europe in the 1980s, and game fishermen quickly recognized their usefulness. At first they were threaded on a hook weighted at the eye to facilitate casting. Now available in all shapes and colors, they

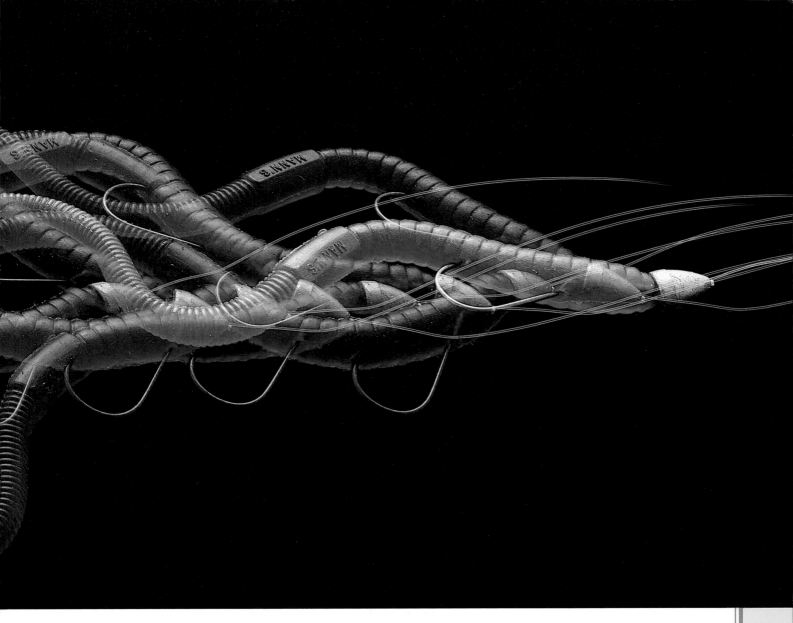

can also achieve excellent results when used on deadbait tackle.

Worm-like, flexible lures are particularly recommended for tempting freshwater bass, perch and pike. The photograph on this page shows how a lure of this kind moves in the water. Its irregular undulations prove irresistibly attractive, even though no real worm would behave in this way. Its movements are more akin to the strugglings of an injured fish. In nature, any animal which behaves abnormally is inevitably eliminated, and culling them is the role of predators. Anglers who can impart this sort of irregular motion to their lures therefore increase their chances of a bite.

Some years ago, in France, flexible lures were responsible for some amazing catches of zander, a close cousin of the walleye. It was not uncommon to take ten or more fish in a morning. Then the bites became fewer and fur-

ther between. At first, anglers thought that the zander had moved on, but fishing different swims produced no better results. This was the repeat of a phenomenon previously observed with trout: when spinners first came on the market, they would throw themselves at the lure with complete abandon; then they got wise. This is clear proof that fish are capable of learning. Familiarity breeds mistrust.

The fisherman should therefore always be prepared to change his lure. The shape, color and vibrations produced by lures act on predatory fish in a way we little understand. Only by experimenting at the water's edge will the angler hit on the right lure. And remember: a model that has given good sport one day will not necessarily do so the next.

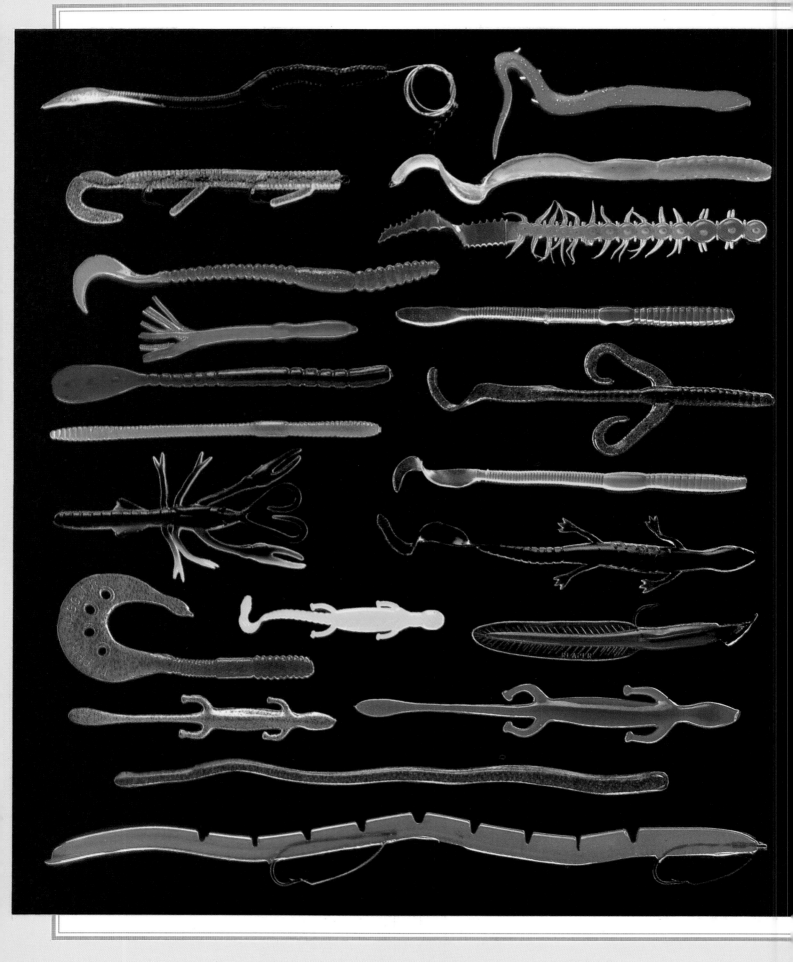

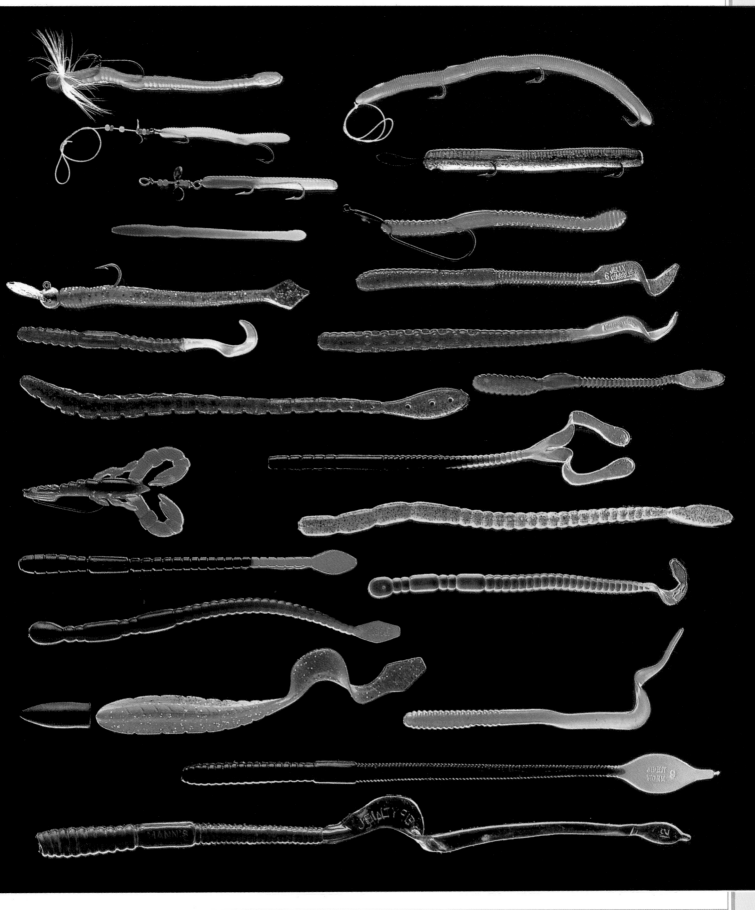

FISHING WITH A FLEXIBLE PLASTIC WORM

This type of lure is widely used in the United States for catching large- and smallmouth bass, though it will also attract other predatory fish, particularly walleyes and pike. It is a tempting bait because the comma-shaped tail wiggles at the slightest movement. Being long and flexible, each pull on the line causes the worm to twist and turn in a way calculated to draw a bass out of ambush.

European fishermen are also beginning to understand the advantages of this lure for other fish, notably zander and large perch. Weighted at the head end, exactly as if it were fixed to deadbait tackle, the worm can be used for exploring the most restricted swims and lies.

Color, as we have noted, is of the greatest importance. A translucent red appears to be effective with all fish, but the fisherman should be prepared to experiment, even with the most garish colors. In the section on sensory perception, we saw how a fish's vision is different from our own: some colors are not perceived, even quite close to the surface, while others remain visible at great depth. This accounts for the fact that fluorescent yellow is highly successful in luring zander, which are well equipped to detect this color in deep water.

Fishing with a flexible worm. Cast over the swim and hold the rod high as the lure drops toward the bottom. By dipping and raising the tip, it is possible to impart short, irregular, up-and-down movements to the lure, which is a good way of tempting the fish.

It is often when you lower the rod and the worm descends to the bottom that the fish will attack. The line should be kept taut, so that you feel the bite. A little slack in the line and the fish is inevitably lost.

FIXING A FLEXIBLE PLASTIC WORM

The lead weight is the spinning lead for a minnow, which should be slipped on to the line before tying the hook. Push the hook through the first three-eighths inch of the worm's "head," with the point projecting slightly.

Pull on the hook, so that the shank emerges and the knot stays hidden inside the head of the worm. Now plant the hook in the body of the worm, keeping the point covered so that it will not snag weed and obstacles.

Pull the weight down against the worm. If it tends to slide, it can be fixed by pinching a small split shot on the line just above it. Remember that the worm must be free to wiggle each time the line is pulled or allowed to go slack.

The time to strike is just after you feel the fish bite. Dip the rod for a split second to let the fish seize the lure, which is a long object to cope with, without snatching it out of its mouth prematurely. This point is most important. Strike energetically. As the point of the hook is buried in the plastic of the lure, it has first to be driven through the worm, then into the jaws of the fish. It may help to strike twice. Once hooked, the fish will make a run for cover. You need a strong line to keep it in open water.

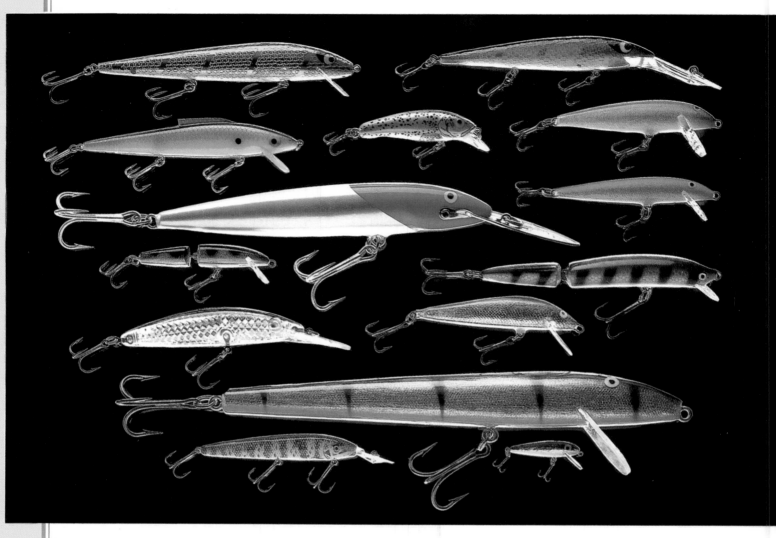

PLUGS

It has been claimed that plugs were invented in Finland, in the early years of the century, by a pike fisherman who observed that these predators do not attack just any fish in a shoal, but those which are sick or injured and therefore swim differently from the others. To imitate their abnormal behavior he fashioned a lure out of pine bark. It was fitted at the front end with a vane designed to impart to the lure the undulating movement characteristic of a crippled fish. The first Rapala was born.

Rapalas are now used all over the world and have been copied, more or less effectively, by many manufacturers. Modern plugs are generally made of plastic or balsa wood. The diving vane is designed to impart the desired motion through the water. The fisherman can adjust the angle to suit, though it is better to leave well alone unless you really know what you are doing.

Some plugs float on the surface and dive down each time the angler pulls on the line. These are suitable for surface-feeding trout, bass, pike and perch. Some are designed for use at mid-depth, while yet others are heavily weighted for plumbing the depths. Some plugs are articulated, to increase the effect of rapid undulation. These are excellent for trolling, but can also be used for fishing from the bank with good casting tackle. They can be jerked through the water to give the impression of life, but this is often not necessary.

SPINNERS

Many types of spinner are now available in the tackle shops, though the more modern lures have never displaced some of the older ones, whose effectiveness has continued undiminished over the decades.

As they rotate, spinners give off vibrations. If they are to excite a predator, these vibrations must fall within a certain frequency range. Quite advanced research to gain understanding of this phenomenon has been carried out by anglers in the United States.

The way a spinner is dressed is also of vital importance. As it turns, the metal spoon reflects colors which may attract the fish. Conventional wisdom has it that a dark-colored spoon is required in clear water, and vice-versa. This is true only in part.

Spinners, especially those intended for use with ultra-light tackle, are often embellished with an artificial fly mounted on a treble hook. This may increase the lure's effectiveness. A tuft of red wool on the treble hook of a pike spinner is known to be a killer. Recently, there have been experiments in replacing the streamer with a flexible lure. This may well work, but it is easy to overlook the fundamental point: the depth at which the spinner moves through the water and the speed with which it can be recovered is determined by the total weight of the lure, and the shape and size of the spoon. There is no chance of catching fish swimming in mid-water if your spinner is operating close to the bottom.

ARTIFICIAL FLIES

The fly is joined to the line by the leader (length of nylon), usually tapered from line to fly and varying according to circumstances from 5 ft or so on brooks to sometimes over 20 ft on lakes. Leaders can be manufactured as single tapers or custom-made by the angler by joining different diameter nylon monofilament. The diameter and breaking strain of the final section will relate to size of fish likely to be encountered, power of tackle used,

incidence of water weed and the size of the fly.

An artificial fly is traditionally constructed of feather, fur, silk, wire and tinsel, but these materials are being increasingly augmented by modern synthetics. The original intent would have been to deceive fish by imitating obviously visible flies noted to be taken from the surface. Problems in flotation would at that stage have led to submerged flies and the discovery that these, under some conditions, could remain effective.

Human ingenuity has extended this range of sculpted fur and feather (still termed "flies") into nearly every form of aquatic food item. Larvae, pupae, and adult stages of aquatic flies, beetles, terrestrial insects, leeches, freshwater shrimps, small fish and even small mammals are represented by "flies".

Tying a spider pattern is relatively simple. Typically these are wingless but the example shown has hackle tip wings which are both light and durable. In appropriate sizes and colors it can be very effective. Correct proportions should be maintained, however, to produce an acceptable silhouette and to enable the fly to sit correctly on the water. The hackle (collar of feather fibers) should be of good quality and wound evenly round the hook. The fibers should be of correct length, approximately the distance from eye of hook to the point, to ensure that the fly is presented at the right angle. The tail fibers also assist in keeping the artificial floating fly in a horizontal, correct position. Ephemeroptera, which this fly represents, actually have either two or three tails according to species, but it is practical in fishing to have up to six – and the fish raise no objection to this surfeit!

Traditionally flies are made using the neck feathers (cape) of a fowl. Those from the cock bird, brighter and stiffer for dry flies and the softer hen hackles for wet (sub-surface) flies. For flies, hackles or wings can be made of either feather or fur, as can fly and nymph bodies. Hackles can be spider style (a collar wound round the hook at the eye), palmered (wound in open turns down the body), as a beard (under the hook) or parachute (wound in a horizontal plane above the hook shank).

The range of patterns is vast and growing. Every fly-tier is a designer and within size limitations every crea-ture a fish may eat will have been represented by a "fly". Further, even when not disposed to feed, predatory fish may exhibit aggression and seize a brightly colored lure with an enticing action. Hence gaudy "fancy" flies and lures – most salmon flies fall into this category.

For staple food items, adult insects represent a fleeting opportunity for the fish, being available only for a few seconds on hatching and again when egg laying. The sub-surface existence presents much greater opportunity either as larvae or free-swimming pupae of the caddis flies and chironomids(mosquito-like flies). These are obviously fished below the surface and moved slowly or, as nymphs or pupae at point of hatching, in the surface film. Takes can be detected visually or felt through the line providing it is not slack.

Lures usually rely upon "life" when they are pulled through the water and normally have long fluttering "wings" made of hair, long hackles or Marabou (soft very mobile fluffy feathers from the turkey). Some lures utilize deer hair spun on the hook and clipped to shape. This makes a light body with excellent floating properties when dressed with a floatant. Often pulled quickly through the water, takes to lures are usually very obvious.

Selection of flies is seasonal. Ephemeroptera ("mayflies") progress through species through the season as do stoneflies. Caddis flies usually come into their own in the summer. Nymphs are constantly available to fish. Lures too can be successful through the season but those that represent small fish are more effective when the quarry are actively feeding on fry – of similar size, in late summer.

HOW TO TIE A SIMPLE SPIDER PATTERN

1 - Tie in the hackle tip wings on top of the shank with the silk (tying thread), supporting the wings in position with turns immediately in front and behind.

working in one direction, a little at a time.
4 - Wind the dubbing in touching turns to form the body, stopping short of the eye, and secure with a few turns of the silk.

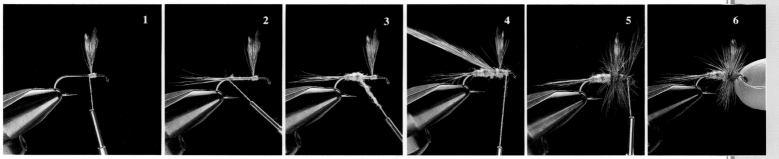

2 - Wind the silk in touching turns down to a point on the shank just above the barb, tying in the tail fiber on top of the shank. Wind the silk back toward the eye, tying in the prepared hackle by its stem behind the wings.
3 - Take the silk back to the bend of the hook and roll the dubbing – teased out of wool or fur – on to the silk with fingers

5 - Wind the hackle round the shank, a couple of turns behind the wing and a few in front. Secure the end of the hackle with several turns of the silk and cut off any surplus.
6 - Finish off the head of the fly with a knot or whip finish, and with a needle point carefully varnish the head for security.

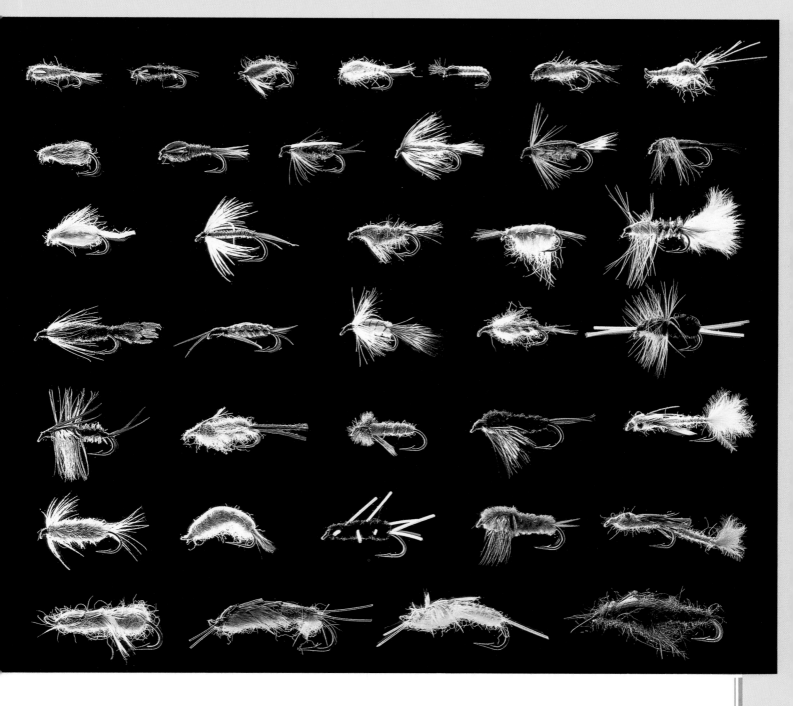

The enormous number of different flies is testimony to the imaginative flair of those who fish with them. The top four rows on the left-hand page illustrate some of the established classics, all made of natural materials. The hackles (neck feathers of a cock or other bird) are tied round the shank of the hook. These flies float perfectly, but do not always settle on the water with sufficient delicacy. The remedy for this is the "parachute" fly (three specimens illustrated in the last row but one, left), which has a horizontal hackle, bound to a perpendicular projection on the shank of the hook. This ensures that the fly always lands gently on the surface, and the right way up.

Though available from dealers, flies of this type are little used due to their fragility. The final row consists of four American-style "no-hackle" flies, which are made entirely of synthetic materials. Extremely simple in design, they nevertheless give good results. It would appear that fish often prefer flies that lie trapped in the surface film.

The page above shows a selection of nymphs, a type of so-called "wet" fly. Though many closely resemble aquatic larvae or pupae, others are highly imaginative in design.

BASS

HENRI LIMOUZIN

Strangely enough, or maybe it was prophetic, the author's first encounter with fishing for the largemouth and smallmouth bass (known as black bass in Europe) was quite modern in style, even though it dates back to those early post-war years in France when he was no more than a boy of thirteen or fourteen.

In those days, hardly a week went by when, together with brothers, and often accompanied by father, the trip would be made, by bicycle of course, to the marshes, some twenty miles from their home town. Fishing was for tench, bream and young carp, but with little interest in flesh-eating fish, species which were as yet beyond the reach of apprentice anglers.

One day, at a favorite fishing spot on the marshes where the canal deepened, an astonishing spectacle unrolled: around a bend in the canal just where it began to widen, came a light boat manned by two anglers dressed in khaki, wearing caps with large square peaks. They were American soldiers, but that was nothing unusual since there was still an American base a few miles away, and military vehicles were for ever crossing the region.

The surprise, however, was the way they were fishing.

Sitting in their aluminum boat, wearing sun-glasses, they were keeping to the middle of the canal and, one on each side, were casting lures into the vegetation along the banks, using short casting rods. The lure they were using was a fantastic rubber frog which, thanks to the quick jerking movements skillfully imparted to it by the anglers, was stretching its legs and jumping like a real frog from one water lily leaf to another! The crowning moment came when, following a noisy boiling of the water, one of the men caught a good-sized fish. Because of the various somersaults it performed before landing in the net, it could be identified without difficulty: it was a "black". And in the same manner, the Americans went on to catch another two or three only a short distance away from the towpath.

One was not to know then, of course, that some decades later one would be fishing for bass American style, and experiencing a pleasure that has never palled. But before reaching that point was a long, circuitous journey, the milestones on which were marked by the catching of hundreds, if not thousands, of pike, perch and zander (related to walleyes), the objects of successive, all-consuming passions for predatory fish.

A superb predator that will reward the angler with great sport.

During this time the occasional encounter with the bass had only served to teach that it was no stranger to our waters.

At that time there was quite a dense population of bass in the marshes which, with their innumerable canals, drains and dikes, channeling slow-moving, warm water, amply supplied with aquatic vegetation, provided this fish with a very favorable habitat, especially since it was able to feast on its favorite prey (larvae and aquatic insects, mollusks, small fry, frogs and, later, its compatriot the American crayfish). Competing species were limited to the pike and the perch, comparatively few in number, the zander still being completely unknown. Only, perhaps, the eel and the Canadian perch, or sun perch, its close cousin and another compa-

triot, which could then be found swimming about in the marshes, were able to impose any serious constraints on the expansion of the bass by swallowing its eggs and fry in their hatching areas, despite the constant and aggressive watch it keeps to protect its offspring from these hungry predators.

Nevertheless it was impossible, in the 1950s and 1960s, to walk alongside the canals of the green Venise and of the marshes without noticing, here and there, bass of all sizes, quite close to the surface, fixed to the spot absolutely motionless in those empty spaces among the bankside vegetation. On some days, three or four looming silhouettes would swim, with undershot jaws, dark shapes half way down in the pale, yellow-green water, gliding along imperceptibly, in perfect formation,

TECHNIQUES FOR FISHING WITH LIVEBAIT

Bass actively seek out small fry to feed on, so it is quite a natural step to offer them living prey as bait. Any light fishing rod (of the trout fishing variety), fitted with a light casting reel of 22-28/100ᵉ will be suitable.

FISHING METHOD: adjust the stop-knot for fishing at the required depth: 12 in or so beneath the surface to begin with. Attach the livebait (a small roach, bleak, perch, rainbow fish, chub, or indeed a minnow, gudgeon or whitebait) by the lips (or the back). Cast this livebait to the chosen spot. Once the float has straightened up, allow the livebait to "work" on its own for a few minutes, then move it slightly, either by lifting the rod or by giving a few turns on the reel. If there is no strike, cast again to another position and

try once more, adjusting the float's stop-knot so as to fish progressively deeper, until the bait is being dragged along the bottom. In running water allow the float to drift, "steering" it alongside obstacles. You may also fish using a ledgering technique.

When a fish takes the bait, release a good length of line before gently winding in. It is important that the livebait remains active: replace it as soon as it becomes motionless at the end of the line. Other livebait can be presented in the same way: crayfish, small lampreys, freshwater shrimps, large maggots, leeches, etc. It should be noted, however, that it is against the law in many countries to use frogs as bait when fishing.

PREVIOUS PAGES *As in the case of their cousins, the perches, the bass species live in shoals, except for the very large specimens which tend to be solitary.*

their pectoral fins being the only part offering any noticeable sign of movement. These were much larger specimens, and they roused such an eager desire that one could hardly resist the temptation to catch one.

Quickly, with the help of our roach line, baited with a microscopic piece of ham from our sandwiches, a bait fish was caught, fry of the sort that continually dart around in the water just beneath one's feet. As soon as one was dangling from our minute hook, without taking the trouble to change the roach line, it was lowered, an improvised livebait to a position just in front of the mouths of the bass, trusting that they would not have disappeared in the meantime! And one fish did actually bite – at least for a few seconds before it broke the pathetic line. Most of the time, however, it must be

admitted that even the most wriggling of small fry left these noble creatures quite indifferent! Even when the bait was moved, as though it were a yo-yo, right under their noses, they would continue to project their disdainful lower lips. In the end they would withdraw, sinking slightly as they did so, until they were lost in the depths of the water.

Then, just for the fun of it, attempts would be made on the more modest specimens near the surface, among the vegetation, where there was more luck: with a sudden snatch, the bait was swallowed whole, and its attacker carried it off with the small float in its wake. This was done with pounding hearts, even though it was a game, a wait before lifting the rod, and soon the small predator was on the grass, a perfect replica of the large

USING THE EARTHWORM

The earthworm is a delicacy as far as bass are concerned. It can be presented on the same mount, and in the same way, as other livebait, but to be effective, and to make fishing more interesting, it is better to use a light 8–9ft rod, which is more flexible and sensitive, fitted with a light fixed spool reel well supplied with 18–14/100e line, and then to proceed as follows.

FISHING METHOD: Choose a large split lead shot depending on the desired fishing depth and the distance to be cast. To fish right at the surface, or just beneath it, among water-lilies for instance, it is possible to dispense with this shot altogether, since the weight of the worm will be enough. Attach a large worm to the shank of the hook. Cast it carefully to the chosen spot and allow it to sink to the required depth (and, if applicable, to drift with the current); then give a few slow tugs to the line by raising the rod in small steps, punctuated by brief rests. Now allow the bait to sink again while lowering the rod and winding in the slack

line with a few turns of the reel. All layers of the water can be tested in this way, starting at the surface (another excellent method is to cast the bait deliberately onto a water lily, for instance, and to make it shake a little before allowing it to fall into the water), and continuing until you reach the bottom. When a fish attacks the bait it is often a sudden movement, particularly when it is near the surface, but it can take place as the worm sinks and is then quite discreet (hence the importance of having a fluorescent yellow thread to identify the slightest stop or movement of the line). Wind in at once when there is any unusual movement, because the bass swallows an earthworm at a truly phenomenal speed.

USING THE PLUG

Having enjoyed a good reputation for its effectiveness for some time now, as far as perch fishing is concerned, the classic plug is able to arouse the same aggressive frenzy among bass, since they are just as curious and aggressive in response to anything that wriggles and shines as their distant relatives. Besides being child's play to use, they also have the advantage of being able to reach anywhere, even among the worst submerged obstacles where any other type of lure would becoming irretrievably tangled. To use them to best advantage, however, it is necessary to fish with a very flexible, or even "slack" at the tip, 10–16ft rod, depending on whether you are fishing from land or from a boat, in conjunction with a light casting reel containing line of 28-30/100e for the more crowded places.

USING SPECIAL LURES

These lures, designed in the United States specially for large- and smallmouth bass fishing, have very recently been introduced to France by the French firm MEPPS which makes flaps to go with them. Our anglers are now in the process of discovering their use for all European predators, and their success is quite remarkable. They combine one or more spinners or spoons with a flexible lure or a tuft of elastic threads, fitted to a weighted hook of the lead-head variety.

FISHING METHOD: This is based on the principle of animation involving each component of the lure in succession. It is therefore a combination of spoon fishing and flexible lure fishing. The method for using each of these special lures is clearly described on the packet.

The working of a dangling lure combined with a spinner blade. The accumulation of several effects is often decisive for attracting a bass.

hunters so coveted. They were returned to the water, giving pleasure despite everything: a small fishing episode using live bait.

MARSH CANALS AROUND THE MOROCCAN LAKES

Angling books and magazines had revealed a great deal about the American bass, their varieties (largemouth and smallmouth), their habits and their behavior, the highly specialized techniques that North American anglers have had to develop in order to catch them, and the incredible fascination this creature has for anglers in the New World. And the chance was yet to come. It came more than forty years after those beginnings in the marsh canals. But what an explosion of excitement when a middle-aged man and this species of fish, with all its power and personality, found themselves in each other's presence! It was not a case of having to feel one's way, and no awkwardness or incomprehension were involved: everything fell into place as though "I had only left yesterday," and the keys acquired from observation, experience, the sharpening of the senses, and the instinct (in the sense that this word is applied to hunting) possessed by the young inexperienced marsh angler were at once adapted to fit the locks that (so weakly!) defended the secrets of the black bass in this Moroccan lake.

"So here I am, at last!" came the thought, as the water's edge was approached, almost painfully conscious and joyful about this imminent encounter, yet tinged with the sudden fear of disappointment. There had been a dream for so long now about the promise of these enormous bass, based on reports received from a friend, reports read and re-read perhaps a hundred times over the space of ten years. However, the fisherman's instinct soon took over. In this new aquatic environment one could identify none of the points of reference so familiar from the marshes at home, and which might have helped locate the bass: only the typical profile and relief of a reservoir, the complete absence of any submerged vegetation, and no surface activity from aquatic fauna. Yet a significant rise in the water level, which had occurred before arrival, had flooded a gentle slope colonized by herbaceous plants and clumps of willows,

The bass usually lies in wait among the vegetation before making its violent attack. A spinner bait is the lure.

the emerging stems of which might provide the type of vegetation cover so loved by the American predator. So it was there that a beginning was made.

Throughout the morning plugs of all types were cast into this aquatic jungle, as well as spoons, and a variety of flexible lures: yet nothing would persuade a bass to rise to the bait. The only specimens noticed, from time to time, were healthy looking schools of small fry, recognizable despite their size. They appeared to be fleeing from some predator, which gave a little hope, but this was soon dashed.

Toward midday, absentmindedly eating lunch under the shade of the eucalyptus trees, realization dawned but without discouragement. It was a case of an old hand needing to discover the secret of the waters before there was any hope of a first catch, especially where such a wild creature as the black bass was involved. One thing was certain: predators were not to be found in the shallows among the flooded vegetation. The old hand would have to look elsewhere.

THREE TURNS OF THE REEL AND SUCCESS!

So one had to follow the course of the bank, fishing rapidly, with the lure slightly submerged. The bank, which was covered with large round pebbles, had quite a pronounced slope; here and there lentanas, which were half submerged by the rising waters, were still quite green and healthy but nothing there either. A number of plugs were lost when they became entangled with their low stems, as well as with the black, submerged skeletons of bushes that had succumbed to previous rising water levels. After the scorching heat of the early afternoon, which caused the air to vibrate in those rocky half craters, covered with thornbushes and euphorbia, at the foot of which stretched small bays which were explored conscientiously, somewhat cooler air developed when the sun, now reaching the hill tops, began to project long shadows across the water. And a light breeze ruffled the surface of the lake.

It was then that, from the corner of one of those rocky shelves which, here and there, served to retain the pebbly slopes, came the surprise of a sudden shoal of some small fish. Quickly the lure was cast to the spot: three turns of the reel and success! A bite. And after an interesting, moderate struggle, with several energetic

CASTING LURES

There is everything to be said for acquiring equipment of the best quality: a carbon casting rod, for instance, that is fine, light and sensitive, 7–8ft in length, and a light fixed spool reel with a reliable, sensitive clutch, holding around one hundred yards of 22-28/100e nylon line.

FISHING METHOD: This depends primarily on the type of lure you have chosen. The spoon: choose from sizes 2 to 4, and begin by exploring the layers closest to the surface, then gradually move downward toward the bottom. In all cases alternate between accelerated movements and slower movements as you turn the reel, and move the rod in a range of directions: spinners which are lead-weighted at their head are often better in deep lakes; spoons which are weighted along their axis are more useful in running water. Good results may also be obtained with the Fluo wriggling lures, 00 to 2.

THE PLUG: there are thousands of varieties of plugs, from the more conventional variety, such as the Rapalas, to the most extravagant examples one finds in well-stocked catalogs. They "work" almost by themselves in the water, thanks to their flaps or fins. The sizes most suited to the bass are 3 to 5 inches. Depending on whether you feel inclined to fish near the surface, at medium depth, or near the bottom,

choose types which dive slightly, moderately or significantly (all of these being floating plugs, of course — which means that when you interrupt retrieval of the line, they start to float toward the surface, a characteristic which has a marked effect in attracting bass); or, if you intend to fish at greater depths, use the "flowing" varieties which sink quite rapidly to the bottom when you stop winding. Vary the speed of recovery, insert pauses of varying lengths, change the direction in which the rod is pointing in order to enhance its sensitivity to the maximum and add considerably to the effectiveness of a lure which would otherwise be drawn in mechanically and in a uniform manner.

THE ARTIFICIAL FROG: this is an imitation frog, made from rubber, foam or floating plastic. By combining tugging and release movements when you retrieve the line, you will cause the frog to extend and then retract its rear legs. It is often fitted with a protected hook to prevent it from becoming tangled with water plants. When the bass is active near the surface, this type of lure is incredibly effective. However, under such conditions you may prefer to use the light casting version of the popper (see whipped lures). There are also flexible plastic frogs that can be used on special mounts (see flexible lures). Finally, manufacturers have recently introduced original lures which combine spoons and flexible lures (see special lures).

The bass feeds readily on crayfish. The small variety, which are easy to come by, make excellent bait.

attempts at an escape, and the inevitable somersaults, a black bass was netted – the first Moroccan bass! It had great symbolic value, and one had no intention in the world of losing it!

Very suddenly the sun disappeared behind the large hill against which the reservoir had been created. At the same time the breeze strengthened and it became decidedly chilly: it was necessary to get back – with six or seven fish of similar size, and perhaps with the first key to what were very new waters.

A PACK IN PURSUIT OF THE PLASTIC WORM

As early as possible the next morning, back at the water, a theory needed testing: the suspicion was that black bass only engaged in active hunting when the sun was hidden behind the hills, in the morning and in the evening, and apart from that only when the light was oblique; this also corresponded to the times when the surface of the lake is agitated by waves. During the day, when the sun is at its height, and the water is as smooth as a mirror, hunting more or less comes to a halt. It is on their own fry – a natural regulatory phenomenon which is common in maintaining a natural balance in waterways – that the bass concentrate their most intense hunting activities; for this purpose they lie in wait at the edge of the rocky shelves that punctuate the pebbly banks, at a depth of three to six feet, on the lookout for the arrival of schools of small fry that follow the contours of the bank. As soon as their prey is within reach,

the attack is waged by a group of five or six hungry and ferocious hunters.

But one does not need to wait for the attack to take place: in order to make a catch one only has to identify these rocky shelves and dangle a lure, after casting a short line parallel to the bank and winding it in until it reaches a good depth. A lot of fish were lost from the hook, but when evening came, one generally ended up with a dozen fish of a good weight which were more than enough to make one happy – at least for the first few days!

This scenario was played out more or less the same every day throughout that first stay. Later on there was the opportunity, during subsequent visits, to verify that this was a constant feature of the lake: in the mornings, until the sun rose above the hill tops, and in the evenings until nightfall, the use of a plug, cast or trailed in areas of comparatively shallow water (up to six or ten feet) almost always resulted in a catch.

However, this does not mean there was nothing one could do during the day itself. Another experience uncovered the trail of a second key to this black bass lake. On the fourth or fifth day, the early-bird routine produced nothing in response to Rapala; this was almost expected because the weather was not the same as usual: there was not the slightest breeze on arrival and, instead of the early-morning coolness, an oppressive, clammy heat, almost storm-like in nature, hung over the mirror-smooth lake.

Toward 11 o'clock, having finally understood that

The flexible lure with a weighted head is excellent for tempting bass. If the hook is pressed into the plastic, this will prevent it from catching on branches.

USING FLEXIBLE LURES

To use these to full effect, the skillful movements of the angler himself are decisive, and these are best demonstrated using a good rod of the deadbait variety (though with a more flexible tip) and a light casting reel holding a good length of Fluo 24-28/100e nylon.

FISHING METHOD: This takes the form of animating the lure in a combination of the light casting fishing method and the vertical, dangling method, causing the flexible lure to jump around in a lively manner on the bottom. To achieve this, once you have cast, wait for

the lead to make contact with the bottom, then raise the rod with small successive fairly sharp tugging movements. When the rod is approaching a vertical position, lower it deliberately, but making sure the line remains tense. At the same time retrieve any slack line; continue in this way until the lure is beneath the rod. It is a good idea to break up this procedure with short pauses, small slides along the bottom, and with accelerated and slowing movements, etc. Strike at once whenever you feel anything unusual. Vary the shapes and colors used if you are not successful.

the Rapala would get nowhere, it was decided to attach a large artificial earthworm to the line, on a hook with notched barbs, to see whether the bass were further out and in deeper waters. No sooner had the plastic lure touched the bottom (estimated at 15 or 20 feet), than a sudden tug was felt on the hook, just like the feel of a zander, walleye or a deadbait. An immediate strike resulted in a fine specimen thrashing around in the depths, before rising like an arrow to the surface with a jump in the air. It continued to struggle furiously as it was steered toward the bank. It was then noticed that it was being closely followed by five or six of its fellows, seeking to rob it of its prey, as fish do!

The catch was quickly brought to safety and the artificial worm cast back to the same spot: it was taken by one of the frustrated pursuers even before it reached the bottom, and this resulted in the same kind of excitement one had grown used to when fishing for zander. Then another catch. This frenzied hunting went on for a good hour, and produced seven or eight fish (because one has to allow for mistakes when winding in and for hooks

working their way loose, which occurred more frequently than with the plugs). This was the first experience of the gregarious hunting habits of the black bass – something that had been familiar in the case of the perch and the zander – and it was a fascinating experience. This frantic activity was to come to an end as suddenly as it had started, but there were to be countless opportunities to relive the experience on subsequent visits.

THE SECRET: FINDING THE RIGHT DEPTH

From that first visit, the challenge of which made success all the more rewarding, the most vivid memory is of two fish in particular, because they were the exception to the behavior just described. Still hoping to find

PREVIOUS PAGES *The bass defends itself with great energy. It thrashes around near the surface and there is a significant risk of it coming off the hook.*

FISHING WITH TIED LURES

The bass is a phenomenal adversary for the fly-fisherman: it attacks surface lures with a spectacular brutality and defends itself with incredible strength, which arouses the fighting instincts in the angler. Just as energetic, if less spectacular, is the way it attacks submerged whipped lures. A good reservoir trout rod will serve well, but if you want more specialist equipment, you will need to acquire a 9–10ft rod for 7–10 line, a W.F. floating line if you want to fish using the popper or other surface lures, and perhaps a sinking

line for fishing at a greater depth using submerged lures; a good length of 12lb Dacron backing provides a suitable margin for maneuver with large specimens, a large manual reel, or better still an automatic one, and a leader made from 5–7ft of 28/100e monofilament line. It now remains to choose some good lures from the immense range offered to us through mail order catalogs. If their color and shape is of some importance, the most important ingredient is the way in which they are manipulated.

some bass that might show interest in a surface lure, some time was spent, each day, trying with a whipped popper. The favorite spot was the narrow and not particularly deep bottom of an inlet formed by a tributary stream, well sheltered from the wind, yet sunny and with a plentiful supply of thornbush branches and submerged lentanas. In the absence of any sign of bass on the surface, one fished the water as one might for trout, using a fly bait, content with the simple pleasures of whipping the hook and carefully positioning the popper alongside some obstacle, before winding in the line with a series of tugs so that it would wriggle enticingly. A fishing colleague was there in the boat, and watched my efforts with the greatest interest as he steered back and forth to assist the venture. Suddenly, just beside a lentana stem, recognized immediately because it had yielded a number of fish there on the previous visit, the distinct sound was heard of an explosion beneath the popper and the capture of a bass, which then started to struggle for all it was worth. It took all one's strength to bring it under control with the assistance of a

companion who prevented the adversary from pulling the boat toward the submerged bushes. In the end it was grasped firmly by the lower jaw, between thumb and index finger, and hauled on board. The next day the same thing happened again, but at another spot with similar sheltering plants.

Even when the bass seems to have gone down to the depths, there is always the hope of finding an isolated specimen at certain spots, waiting to be caught using surface fishing methods. This was another useful lesson to learn, but the lake still had other secrets.

Before reaching this high point, however, it must be admitted that there was no escaping some days when the fish just would not bite, in contrast with other days when fishing was all too easy using a given technique. One had to try all the classic methods for bass fishing in order to catch some large specimens. Faithful to its widespread reputation among American anglers, the "achigan" (the Canadian name for the European black bass) would respond to anything: livebait, metal lures, spinners, flies and streamers, flexible plugs and imita-

TIED LURES

The most amusing of these are the poppers which, with their chamfered balsa heads at the front, disturb the water each time the line is tugged, while their elastic threads quiver each time they pause.

However, one can also present real dry flies or submerged flies: streamers, muddlers, bucktails, hairbugs and zonkers.

FISHING METHOD: With the lure in position, wait a short while and then cause it to quiver slightly where it is. Now give a sharp tug on the line, so that the pop-

per disturbs the water. Start all over again raising the rod very slowly to an angle of around 45°. Allow another short pause, then lower the rod, winding in the slack line, and repeat. Do not accelerate retrieval by increasing the number of rapid tugs in order to make the lure "pop," because it is often during the pause that the predator will attack.

When you see an "explosion" near the surface, wait momentarily before striking sharply. With submerged lures, use the same technique as for reservoir trout.

tions of all types, poppers, fly spoons, and so on any-thing that moved along, vibrated, swam, wriggled, turned, somersaulted or moved in any other way, might be attacked by this aggressive fish.

BASS CONCENTRATING ON LARGE RED DRAGONFLIES

In that same Moroccan lake livebaits were fished (small barbel and, of course, black bass!), presented on rudimentary lines, but right alongside the most dense of submerged obstacles, which provided its permanent contours. Not the most exciting of fishing experiences, but a more or less constant success seemed guaranteed, and it was possible to select the largest specimens. Without great conviction spinners were tried and spoons too: the result was a consistent success in the evenings in the shallows, but the catch rate was only moderate and often limited in deeper water, where the larger, but rarer, specimens were to be found. Jointed metal fish dangled right in the middle of obstacles that were inaccessible to any other form of lure: a fast, effective method of fishing and exploring a stretch of water, with immediate catches if any fish were present. Flexible lures of all shapes and colors, on the widest variety of mounts, or used in association with the most sophisticated of American metal lures (Bass Killer, Mean Dude, Timber Doodle, etc.), fish were caught with all of them. There was also constant success using deadbait. The only tested technique that remained to be tried out more fully and seriously was the use of flies, streamers and whipped bucktails, at different depths.

In order to rediscover the intensity of the past experience, it was necessary to think back to the situation as it had been exactly one year earlier, that is to say in early November. On arrival, no time was lost in discovering that the black bass were concentrating their attention on the abundant large red dragonflies which flitted around just above the surface of the water, occasionally landing on the low stems of the lentana. Now and then a bass would jump out of the water, with a resounding splash, in order to snap at one of them. Since fly rods happened to be included in the equipment this activity caused great excitement, beyond expectations. It took a few days to develop the right tactics, but the first bass caught using the whipped popper was one of those unforgettable fishing experiences.

Fishing began in the place where other methods had regularly succeeded, but it was not long before it was discovered that it was more exciting to stalk the bass directly as they pursued their own prey, the dragonflies. As soon as the sound of disturbed water occurred among the dry and half submerged lentana bushes, an approach was made by rowing across to the spot as quietly as possible (or on foot along the bank). Once a good position had been reached for casting, the necessary length of line was released and the popper cast to the point just beside the stems where the movement had occurred. After leaving the lure motionless for some seconds, and as the ripples it had created widened, it was moved with small jerking movements, winding in the line in rapid sweeps of a fairly generous length. Quite often it had moved hardly a yard before it was pounced on fiercely in a swirl of water projected by a predator that had been floating just beneath the surface. Almost at once the hook was firmly embedded in the mouth of the fish.

One did not always come out of this encounter the winner, but it was a challenge accepted and earnestly followed through, almost causing one's heart to burst when it was a really large beast. However, often – after a number of excursions, some mastered better than others – it ended with a grip on the lower jaw of the defeated party, and its being raised above the head of the victor in triumph, to the acclaim of his companions. This particular way of holding black bass has, in recent times, been frowned upon and is gradually and quite rightly being abandoned.

At this stage in the learning curve it was easy to give an ungrudging testimonial to the black bass, even though achievements had been modest in comparison with those of American largemouth bass anglers or some European black bass specialists. In many cases the latter have fished for the species for decades.

To sum up the superb qualities of this amazing predator: it takes the angler into another world of unforgettable moments and, eventually, a deep nostalgia.

From that first visit to the lake it was felt that something exceptional in angling would be experienced.

A floating lure under attack at the surface. The water lilies along the edges are excellent places to find bass.

A SQUAD OF SMALL BASS LOOKED ABOUT TO ATTACK A RAPALA

One of the group was fishing using a floating Rapala. He had only just begun to retrieve his line, alternating release movements, which enabled it to rise to the surface, with accelerated movements, causing it to dive six inches or so, when his lure was pursued by a squad of small bass which looked about to attack it. Suddenly the squad dispersed, and there was the unmistakable attack of a fish the same size as the ones caught previously: between one and two pounds. This entertaining scene continued for a while.

At the same time, some distance away, in a boat, other anglers in the group were fishing, using a flexible lure on a very lightly weighted Drachko-type mount. It was the same story: whether they used a double-tail, a frog or a small fish with a tail fin, they did not have to wait long before they caught their first two-pounder which, like the others, lined up to perform the usual celebratory somersault.

It was then noticed that each time one of these average-sized fish was on the line, and it began to perform the battle routine which we all found so captivating, suddenly, from out of nowhere, there would arrive a commando unit of four or five large predators who would eagerly watch what was going on above them, just like sharks when they pick up the scent of blood. All at once it was realized that what interested them was not the miniature lures, nor the small bass, but the medium-sized fish struggling at the end of the lines!

So out of curiosity, and for amusement, the next catch was given free reign at the end of the line. In an attempt to escape it shook its head from side to side, causing it to disrupt the flow of its natural swimming motion. That was the signal! With the speed of a deer the largest member of the squad sprang at it, and its enormous open jaws devoured the smaller fish. The line was left slack for a moment, and then contact re-established. The predator was securely hooked, and a cautious retrieval began in the hope that it had swallowed its generous-sized prey deeply enough not to be able to regurgitate it before it was landed. And this was indeed the case: it was not long before it was held by the lower jaw, a superb fish weighing around seven pounds. It was not even possible to see the tail of the improvised livebait in its throat; this was hardly surprising since we had already had the opportunity to discover that it was possible to place a whole fist inside the mouth of these larger specimens.

To catch a large bass, using livebait in the form of a medium-sized bass, only just caught by means of a popper on a fly-fishing rod, was rather an unusual occurrence! But apart from its anecdotal nature, this experience provided the key to this creature's predatory behavior, and its discovery was thrilling. This knowledge was put to good use, in various ways, during the week that followed, a week that is one of the most memorable of fishing experiences.

One unusual evening is remembered in particular when, well into the night, repeated walking up and down beside a shallow inlet, resulted in one bass after another, just as one might hunt for trout on those evenings when one strike follows immediately on the heels of another. Hardly had the previous catch been returned to the water when, some distance off, the surface of the black water would erupt as a fish pursued some prey known only to itself. As the ripples widened one would hasten in that direction, release the necessary length of line, and cast the popper to the spot where the movement had occurred. A few playful tugs on the line, and there was the hoped-for explosion, yet each time it was exhilarating. A strike, a fierce struggle with a vicious, leaping fish which would then settle among the vegetation along the bank, waiting for the angler's approach, with the water half way up one's thighs, so that the hook could be removed and the fish carried to dry land.

That evening the atmosphere was absolutely magical and other-worldly, in that moonlit landscape inhabited only by creatures locked together in a frantic battle. In this way some twenty fish were caught, and then back to earth, somewhat dazed from this breathtaking foray into one of the less common of human experiences. The night had swallowed up everything around, and all that remained of the world was its infinite sky, sprinkled with stars.

Leaps performed by bass are always spectacular. It is necessary to release a certain amount of line to prevent it breaking.

LARGEMOUTH BASS

Many of the methods described for bass fishing apply in general to the six freshwater species, but this section is designed to cover specifically the largemouth bass which, in North America, is pursued by more anglers than any other game fish.

Largemouths were originally found only east of the Mississippi River and south of the Great Lakes. But as bass fishing grew in popularity, so did stocking programs. Largemouths are now caught in waters throughout the continental United States and Hawaii, in addition to southern Canada and most of Mexico, and also have been introduced into Europe, Asia, Africa and South America.

The largemouth bass is the largest member of closely-related fishes, called black bass. Others include the smallmouth, spotted, redeye, Suwannee and Guadalupe. The largemouth is distinguished from all of these species by a jaw that extends beyond the eye. All black bass belong to the sunfish family, but differ from sunfish because of their longer bodies.

Largemouths inhale small foods. The bass opens its mouth quickly to suck in water and the food. It then forces the water out the gills while it either swallows or rejects the object. Bass can expel food as quickly as they inhale it, so anglers must set the hook immediately when using small lures or baits.

Bass usually grab large prey, then turn the food to swallow it headfirst. This explains why anglers who use large golden shiners, frogs or salamanders wait a minute or two before setting the hook.

Although bass in the south grow and mature faster, they rarely live as long as largemouths, in colder, northern lakes. In southern waters, bass occasionally reach ten years of age; in northern waters, bass may live as long as fifteen years.

Female bass live longer than males, so they are more apt to reach a trophy size. In one study, 30 percent of the females were five years or older, while only 9 percent of the male bass were five years or more.

Largemouths spawn when the water reaches 63^0 to 68^0 F and temperatures remain within this range for several days. Cold fronts may cause water temperatures to drop relatively sharply, which will interrupt and delay the spawning.

LINE: almost all spin-fishermen and bait-casters use monofilament line. A few prefer braided dacron when fishing in heavy cover. The lightest mono possible for existing conditions should be used. Light line results in more strikes because it is less visible, allows better lure action and can be cast further. But light line may not be strong enough to land a largemouth which has run to thick cover.

PLASTIC WORMS: when asked to choose their favorite lure, the majority of anglers at a national bass-fishing championship named the plastic worm. The lure is effective because of its tantalizing, lifelike action. And when inhaled by a bass, the worm's soft body feels like natural food.
Plastic worms work best in warm water. They can be retrieved through thick weeds or brush without snagging, float over shallow cover or jig along effectively in deeper water.

SPINNERS: the outstanding success of the spinner proves that a lure does not have to imitate natural bass food. A spinner attracts bass with its flash, action and color. These qualities, combined with its semi-snagless design, make it a favorite among anglers who fish weedy or brushy waters.
The spinner combines two excellent lures, the spinner and the jig. The wire shaft resembles an open safety pin. It has a lead-heads jig on the lower arm and one or two spinners on the upper arm.

CRANKBAITS: for best results, a crankbait should wobble freely. The line should be attached to a split-ring or snap or tied on the lure with a loop knot such as a bowline. Snugging the knot directly to a fixed eye will reduce the lure's action, especially when using heavy line.

TOPWATER LURES: Surface, or "topwater", lures work best on calm summer mornings and evenings when bass are feeding in the shallows. They are not as effective in water below 60° F or when the surface is fairly rough.
Topwater lures may be the only solution for catching bass nestled under thick mats of vegetation. The commotion often attracts bass even though they cannot see the lure. In this type of cover, anglers sometimes catch bass during midday.
Surface lures also work well for night fishing. Bass may not be able to see a deep-running lure. But they can detect the noise and vibration of a topwater lure. And when they move closer, they can see its silhouette against the moonlit sky.

JIGS: bass that ignore fast-running plugs will often strike lures jigged vertically near their hiding spots. Jigging lures, including lead-head jigs, jigging spoons, vibrating blades and tailspins, are a good choice when fishing in deep water.

LIVEBAIT: the overwhelming majority of bass fishermen use artificial lures. But there is no doubt that livebait works better in many bass-fishing situations. Trophy bass hunters swear by livebait. A glance at the record book shows that the second largest bass was taken on a crayfish and the third largest was caught on a nightcrawler.
Largemouths are more apt to strike livebait after a cold front, or when the water temperature is above or below their active feeding range. Sluggish bass grab only slow-moving food. But some artificial lures lose their action at slow speeds. Livebait, however, can be inched along the bottom or dangled from a bobber. Lethargic bass take more time to examine their food, so they are more likely to be suspicious of and therefore ignore an imitation.

LURE SELECTION: at the end of the day an angler on a new water may have been selecting lures on a trial-and-error basis, sometimes without an option. Generally, however, allowances should be made for the depth of the swims, for example, not only with respect to the depth itself, but as to whether the fish will be deep or shallow. Fishing thick cover, such as sunken brush, may need a lure that is relatively snag-free, such as a spinner or plastic worm rigged Texas style. Sometimes an active or noisy lure may be needed to trigger a response, especially if the largemouths are in the preferred feeding band of 60°–80° F. At higher or lower temperatures a smaller, slow-moving lure should be selected and a livebait in cold water. There is some debate about lures for clear water and high light levels: some anglers prefer bright lures (as for rainbow trout), but black or purple plastic lures also achieve good results.

FEEDING PATTERN: the inexplicable in largemouth fishing can be summed up by saying that however the condition can be interpreted there is certain to be a feeding pattern: a time of day: a mode of attack. To be successful at catching largemouths the fisherman needs to be adept at identifying this feeding pattern. The difficulty is that the pattern may change daily (even during the day) but may hold for weeks during stable weather. Feeding periods may be very short; and deep-water bass may be difficult to suss out, other than with slow-moving traits or lures.

COLD FRONTS: few anglers agree as to why bass fishing slows down after a cold front. But all agree that it does slow down. And if the cold front is severe, bass may not bite for several days.

Some fishermen blame the poor fishing on a rising barometer. But studies have failed to confirm that barometric pressure alone has any effect on fishing. Falling water temperature may have some impact. Even though the air temperature may change drastically, the water temperature changes little.

HOT WEATHER: there are many reasons for poor bass fishing during hot weather. Most signifcant is the abundant food supply. Baitfish hatched in spring reach a size attractive to bass in mid-summer. With natural food so easy to find, artificial lures have less appeal. Mid-summer finds sunlight penetration at its highest. With the sun directly overhead, bass must move deeper or find thick cover. If the water temperature exceeds 80° F, bass look for cooler water in the depths, around springs or near coldwater tributaries. If they cannot find water cooler than 80° F, they become sluggish and eat very little.

CLEAR WATER: largemouths in clear lakes bite best at dusk or dawn, and on windy or overcast days when light penetration is at a minimum. Fishermen on some crystal-clear lakes catch the majority of their bass at night, especially in summer.

Fast retrieves work best in clear water. A slow retrieve gives bass too much time to inspect the lure. The lightest line possible should be used, depending on prevailing conditions.

MURKY WATER: the fisherman who finds a patch of murky water in a clear lake may salvage an otherwise wasted trip. But more often than not, murky water can mean trouble.

Murky water results from muddy runoff, heavy blooms of algae or plankton, rough fish that root up the bottom or the roiling action of large waves. Many shallow, fertile bodies of water remain muddy year-round. Fishing surveys show that anglers catch bass at a significantly slower rate in extremely muddy water. To check water clarity, tie a white lure to the line, lower it into the water and note the depth at which it disappears. If the lure can be seen at a depth of 12 inches or more, chances are that bass can be caught.

FLUCTUATING WATER LEVELS: a rise in water level causes any fish, including bass, to move shallower; a drop pushes them deeper. Fluctuations affect largemouths in shallow water more than bass in deep water. And a rapid rise or fall has a greater impact on fish movement than a gradual change.

Water levels change very quickly in a river following a heavy rain. Bass will respond immediately by moving into flooded vegetation near the bank. But even a slight drop in the water level will send them scurrying to deep water, an instinctive response to avoid being trapped in an isolated pool.

SPAWNING BASS: fishermen continually debate the ethics of catching bass on their spawning beds. Most states allow fishing during the spawning period. But some anglers believe that catching spawners is detrimental to the long-term welfare of the bass population. Wherever such fishing is legal, many anglers voluntarily return their bass.

RIVER FISHING: fishing success on streams is more consistent than on most waters. Cold fronts have less effect on streams and bass continue to bite through summer. Flowing water does not become as warm as standing water and low oxygen levels are rarely a problem.

Fishermen who know how to read the water can easily spot likely holding areas. Bass rarely hold in fast current. They prefer to lie in slack water below some type of obstruction.

Prime bass locations include eddies, log jams, deep pools and undercut banks.

They sometimes feed in a shallow riffle, but usually find a rock to break the current.

NIGHT FISHING: bass seldom move far from their daytime haunts to reach nighttime feeding areas. Look for shallow shoals adjacent to typical midday locations. To avoid spooking bass in these shallow areas, place a marker during the day. Then sneak in to position the boat in the precise spot after dark.

Night fishing is generally best in summer, especially after a warm, still day with clear skies. On windy, overcast days, bass feed during the day so they may not feed again at night.

Most night fishermen use dark-colored lures that create turbulence or vibration. But some anglers swear by plastic worms. Try surface lures first to catch the active feeders. Then switch to deeper-running lures and work a break leading to deep water. Some fishermen attach a snap to the line, so they can change lures easily without retying.

A slow, steady retrieve works best at night, because bass use their lateral line to home in on the lure. If an erratic retrieve is used, the fish may miss.

PIKE

PIERRE AFFRE

The story of the pike belonging to Emperor Frederick Barbarossa, as it has been handed to us by the great Lacépède in his monumental *Natural History of Snakes, Fish and Cetaceans*, at the end of the 18th century, served to ratify one of the great scientific mysteries of all time:

"In 1497 a pike measuring around twenty feet in length, and weighing almost 400lb, whose skeleton has been preserved in Mannheim Cathedral, was caught in Kaiserlautern near Mannheim. It bore the gilt copper ring that had been attached to it by order of Emperor Frederick Barbarossa 267 years earlier. This monstrous fish had therefore lived for almost three centuries." Lacépède's account ends: "What an enormous quantity of fish smaller than itself it must have devoured to sustain its enormous mass over that long lifetime." If this story now causes us to smile, it has not diminished all sorts of legends and superstitions that have grown up around the size and voracity of the *Esox lucius* over the course of the intervening two centuries. In fact the skeleton exhibited in Mannheim Cathedral was a fake, made up from a number of added parts: someone had simply added an impressive number of vertebrae to

those the fish had originally. But if this freshwater Methuselah never actually existed (as we will see, in our climate the pike cannot be expected to live longer than 12–13 years), palæontologists tell us that our friend *Esox* is certainly a living fossil, being a fish that has evolved little and survived almost unchanged for twenty million years. Unchanged except on one point: that of its size, because one of its known ancestors, *Esox lepidotus*, whose fossilized imprint has been found in Siberian shale deposits, measured almost 16 ft in length and weighed at least 880lb. Allowing for the intervening millions of years, then, Lacépède was not all that wrong, and this prehistoric pike must really have caused the other inhabitants of the Tertiary waters to quake and become rapidly extinct.

At the present time the geographic distribution of the species *Esox lucius* is holo-arctic, that is to say it is found in the northern hemisphere and in all the countries that surround the Pole. In Europe, its area of distribution starts on the French slopes of the Pyrenees (only recently has it been introduced to Spain) and extends all the way to the other side of the Ural mountains in northern Siberia. It is present in the Baltic Sea, the low salt

One of the largest freshwater predators, the pike is essential for a healthy ecology in waters inhabited by the cyprinidae.
FOLLOWING PAGES *It feeds for the most part on quite large prey, but this does not prevent it showing an interest in other types.*

content of which is to its liking, and in all Scandinavian countries, as well as in the British Isles. In Ireland it is said to have been introduced by the monks. Its name in Gaelic means: foreign fish. In Northern America it is called the northern pike, to distinguish it from the other four species of pike that populate the waters of that continent. It is found from one side of that continent to the other, from Alaska to Quebec, across the whole of Canada and the United States. Although it also reaches impressive sizes in those countries (but not as large as in Europe), it should not be confused with the maskinonge, or giant North American pike, which is a distinct species, *Esox maskinongy*, very similar in fact to the Siberian pike, *Esox reicherti*. In modern times the latter two fish still reach 80lb in weight and, in their natural habitats, will even attack adult beavers.

Even European pike, however, may reach record weights. Quite recently that august body, the I.G.F.A. (International Game Fish Association) refused to acknowledge a 62lb Swiss pike, not because the fish in

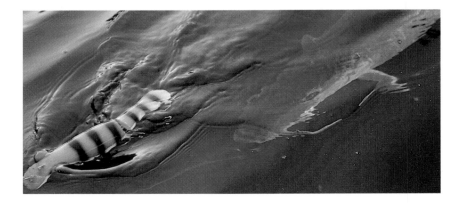

CATCHING PIKE USING THE POPPER

The pike is a predator that is naturally conditioned to take notice of what is happening on the water surface, or at least what is happening above it in the water. The position of its eyes, high in its skull, means that its lateral vision is monocular, but that its vision upward is excellent. When lying in wait, even in very shallow water, the pike keeps to the bottom, slightly inclined toward the surface. Furthermore, this fish has a number of sensory pores beneath the jaws and on its skull, and these are connected via nerves and canals to the lateral line, acting as advance listening stations. Within a radius of several yards, therefore, the slightest change in pressure in the water mass surrounding it will be detected and possibly identified as prey. As in the case of the shark, a swimmer thrashing around on the surface will attract this predator far more readily than an underwater swimmer: a lure used to create a disturbance on the surface is sometimes far more likely to "rouse" a pike at a considerable distance than a spoon or a deadbait at medium depth. The sound of a popper or of an artificial jointed fish clearly arouses the aggressive instinct or curiosity of a fish, and provokes it into biting even when it is not hungry. In this way, using a large surface plug, I have caught an 8lb female in whose throat it was just possible to see the tail of a 2lb pike. Moreover in the summer months, even if it lives essentially on the flesh of other fish, the pike likes to vary its menu, and is not averse to the occasional frog found swimming around on the surface of ponds.

Practically unknown in France, surface lures are used widely in the United States to fish for largemouth bass, muskie and northern pike, the counterpart of the European pike. These lures are of two types: poppers, other sound-emitting surface plugs, and artificial jointed fish. Usually of a substantial size, and made from cork, balsa wood or polystyrene, the front face of poppers is either truncated or slightly concave, so that it will plunge a little when pulled, emitting its characteristic noise (pop pop), and then resurface at once, after making an exciting whirl in the water. In contrast with metal lures, or even plugs, poppers and other surface plugs will often be attacked when they have been completely immobile for some seconds, perhaps in this way imitating the behavior of a frog swimming on the surface. The best method is to throw the popper near an obstacle from which one hopes to draw out a pike: water plants, half submerged branches, sluice-gates, or even open, shallow water where the bottom is matted question had been incorrectly weighed, or because the scales were defective, but simply because it had been caught in a net by a professional fisherman and then sold alive to an angler who released it into a gravel pit on his land and subsequently "re-caught" it using rod and line. This Swiss angler, whose misdeeds were recounted in a number of fishing sport magazines, had apparently "caught" three pike weighing over 40lb in the same way in less than three years. Evidence, at least, that even today Swiss lakes harbor some interest-

ing surprises. Still on the subject of large pike, we should mention here the detective work, worthy of Sherlock Holmes, carried out by an English angling journalist specializing in pike, Fred Buller. In an extraordinarily well-documented book, *Mammoth Pike*, he has reported the evidence of pike catches in excess of 35lb, the minimum weight required for appearing on the list. (He admits that he himself does not appear on the list, since his own record was "only" 32lb.)

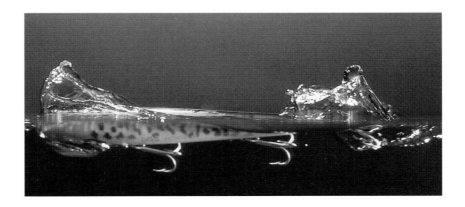

with water plants. You then wait a few seconds, until the ripples created by the lure striking the water have spread out, and with a sharp tug on the rod cause the lure to move a little. It should not move more than 12 inches during this first pull, and should reappear at once with its characteristic popping or gulping sound. If there is no response after an interval of 5–6 seconds, when the water is smooth again make the popper jump a little on the spot with little movements of the rod, before continuing to retrieve the line in the same way, interspersed with pauses and periods of lively movement. The attack on a surface plug by a pike is rarely a discreet affair. Nine times out of ten you can expect quite a show, either in the form of a loud satisfying splash, or because the fish has jumped fully out of the water.

The artificial jointed fish will be attacked in the same way. However, this lure may be retrieved slowly alongside water plants, along banks, or it may be pulled along behind a slow-moving boat. In this case the attack may be less spectacular. When trailing a lure slowly through the water, it is necessary to keep a close watch on the V-shaped wake which it leaves behind it. If the surface of the water is smooth, you

will sometimes notice a second wake some 6–10 inches behind the first. This is a stalking pike. Stop trailing the lure and move it around on the spot; you may not have long to wait. If, on the other hand, the surface of the water is rippled by a light breeze, a stalking pike will "break" the surface ripples, pushing water along behind the lure and creating a momentary smooth patch at that point.

Fishing with surface lures has the advantage that it can be practiced in the summer months when, in many ponds, the full growth of water plants makes it impracticable to use other fishing techniques.

A 92lb pike killed with blows from an oar

The largest pike reported were all supposedly caught in Ireland, where the gentle, temperate climate and the rich limestone lakes encourage extraordinary growth. In 1832 a gardener is said to have used an oar to kill a 92lb pike as it was spawning in the moat around Portumna Castle. Thirty years later, in 1862, John Naughton, fishing with a rod and line in the Derg lough (where the author had the pleasure of fishing last year, but caught nothing over 15lb), is claimed to have caught a 90lb pike. In 1927, again in Ireland, *The Field* informs us that a 90lb fish was caught in the river Shannon. Even though the investigations carried out by Buller were as thorough as one could wish, it is felt that these catches, made so long ago now, should be treated with a certain amount of skepticism! Indeed, another writer on pike in Britain and Ireland, Barrie Rickards, has relegated such captures over 60lbs in Ireland to the realms of mythology. There is, in his opinion, no authentic report of a 60lb fish in Britain or Ireland. He would not dream of extending that statement to apply to other countries. As far as 60-pounders go, be it in Switzerland, or certain other countries in Europe, there can be no doubt about the accuracy of some reports, and Buller has even reproduced photographs of some of these monsters in his book. Berg, the well-known Soviet ichthyologist, provides us with information, in his work *The Freshwater Fish of the USSR*, which relates to species in that part of the world, on a 77lb pike caught near Leningrad in 1930, and corroborated by a report from the Leningrad Institute. We see, then, that our pike is able to reach exceptional weights. Moreover, in France the current record is of 57lb: every month, all over France, pike of between 20 and 30lb are caught. It is all the more baffling, therefore, why France imposed a legal fishing size of only 15 inches, corresponding to a weight of 1–1½lb, on pike caught in French waters. At that size most of these "tiddlers" will not even have reproduced. Yet we wonder why the species is becoming rare in the lakes and public waterways of our country.

In Europe the pike reproduces in spring, between mid February and the end of April, depending on the region. On high ground, spawning may not take place until June. It is the water temperature which is the deciding factor when it comes to the migration that precedes reproduction. In fact the journeys made by pike, though modest in terms of distance, i.e. a few thousand or just several hundred yards, are nevertheless migrations in the true sense of the word. In other words both the males and the females strike out in search of areas rich in vegetation, not too deep, which warm up quickly beneath the pale rays of the winter sun. Along the banks of lakes and ponds, flooded islands, low-lying areas of land submerged by spring floods, marshland, backwaters overgrown with trees and tangled roots, shallows, creeks and even drainage ditches – all serve as excellent environments for pike to reproduce in. Though the presence of vegetation is essential, when it comes to the point of reproduction pike show little discrimination in terms of the surface on which they lay their sticky eggs. Since genuine water plants will not have fully developed at this time of year, it is submerged land-based vegetation of the herbaceous variety which will be used as a nursery for the fry. Thus owners of bare steep-sided gravel pits are advised to provide clumps of fir or broom branches in the shallower, sunny areas if they want to encourage pike to reproduce in their waters.

The female, surrounded by several small males who line up to assist with the fertilization process, moves about a great deal and lays her eggs over large areas. In contrast with the salmonidae, or with zander (related to the walleye), which clean the area in which they intend to lay their eggs, pike pay no particular attention when choosing a place for this purpose. This means there is a great risk if the waters are made cloudy. It only takes some disturbance in the water, depositing a film of mud on the eggs, and they are likely to be suffocated. The other great risk to which fry are exposed is a sudden lowering of the water level which has the disastrous effect of drying out the spawning grounds.

If all goes well, the fry, which take anywhere between a few days and a few weeks to hatch, depending on the water temperature, will then remain fixed to the grasses or submerged plant stems until absorption of the yolk sac is complete (around twelve days on average). As soon as they reach the free-swimming stage they become very active feeders on the zooplankton present in their immediate environment. At the second stage, and this takes place very quickly, the tiny fish give their attention to catching the larvae of insects and other microinvertebrates. Finally, when they reach the age of two to three months, they have become completely fish-eating. But since the other species of fish,

The pike may attack surface lures. It is a fish that is very active at all levels.

USING EXTRA-LARGE LURES TO CATCH BIG PIKE

Once it reaches a weight of 6lb, a pike is already quite capable of swallowing a 2lb roach. When it reaches 10lb, it may make a meal of 3–4lb pike. And when, at the age of eight or nine years, it reaches 20lb in weight, few living creatures occupying the same space are safe. Once it has passed the 30lb barrier, which in food-rich environments (reservoirs, large gravel pits which are connected to rivers, ponds in open country, etc.) may be reached after their tenth year, there are very few lures or types of bait used by the casual angler which have any chance of attracting such large fish. In Great Britain, where there are specialists who fish for nothing other than pike weighing over 20lb (the famous specimen pike, which are then dutifully returned to the water once they have been weighed, measured and photographed), the livebait used has, on occasion, been of pike of nearly 5lb. There is nothing surprising about this, and at a number of private waters in France more than one angler worthy of the name has accounts of a very large pike attacking a good-sized younger pike that was thrashing around at the end of a line.

To take the view, then, that a Lusox No. 3 is the largest size plug to be used for the pike, which is what almost all anglers do think, is a mistake – that is to say a mistake of proportions. A spoon of this size rarely catches young pike, i.e. one weighing less than half a pound, and may on occasions attract a good specimen weighing several pounds. But it is only rarely that such a small lure will cause a really big pike to attack. British studies on pike and their prey, have shown that

after a certain size, over 15lb, the large females (the males never exceed 10–12lb) tend to specialize in catching the males of their species. This specialization in their feeding habits in part explains the fantastic growth of these fish. By consuming protein identical to that from which their own tissue is formed, assimilation is more or less complete, as is the rate of metabolic conversion. And even if the pike is far from being the insatiable ogre of our waters, devouring the equivalent of its own body weight each day, it has to make the maximum use of the food it swallows and not waste its energy, or at least not waste its energy pursuing prey inappropriate to its size. Nutritional experts have recently calculated that an adult pike consumes, on average, four to five times its own body weight in fish and other aquatic animals each year. This explains why anglers have grown accustomed to the long periods of inactivity displayed by this fish.

It is, therefore, necessary sometimes to use extra large lures to catch big pike. By this is meant a lure or bait that represents prey of at least half a pound. At this size spinners have one major drawback: they pull too much on retrieval. This can be easily remedied by mounting two spinners in tandem, or by having the mount followed by a larger rubber fish than those normally sold under the name minnow spoons. But it is mainly by using the range of spoons and spinners, of the Rapala or Creek Chub variety, that the angler is likely to have most success. The larger spoons, more usually reserved for lake fishing and sea fishing, in their

so-called "light," i.e. flatter, version, are perfectly suited to pike fishing, provided one or two trebles are
added (the only modification permitted in lakes and
other self-contained waters, or abroad), because, in
contrast to the fish for which they are specifically
designed (tunny, caranx and barracuda), the pike
almost always attacks them from the side. When it
comes to plugs, choose the types normally used for
sea fishing, showing preference for those that pull least
on retrieval.

Finally there are the surface lures, of the "big-big" variety by Ragot, or others of a jointed cigar shape, which
may be tried out in summer months. These are the
lures used across the Atlantic for catching most of the
record muskies, the giant North American "pike,"
famed in their original habitat for attacking adult
beavers. In this connection it should be pointed out
that in France adult coypu weighing over 6lb have been
found in the stomachs of large pike, though this does
not prove that they were alive when swallowed. It may
be true that this fish will attack adult ducks swimming
on the surface. An angler reports that while fishing on
a lake in France he became aware of game being driven
toward a pheasant shoot in the neighboring woods. A
magnificent cock pheasant, shot as it flew over the oak
trees that surrounded the lake, continued its downward flight toward a point in the middle of the lake,
some fifty yards away from the boat. A few seconds'
rowing would have retrieved a roast for little effort.
But while he was about 15 yards from the unfortunate
floating bird, which was flapping its wings helplessly on

the surface, a pike which must have weighed at least
30lb, swallowed it in one gulp, and all that was left ten
seconds later were a few tail feathers which floated to
the surface. Neither large Rapalas nor a shoe-horn
spoon, would attract the attention of this large bird-
eating monster. This example may give some idea of
the size of lure you need to attach to the end of your
line to catch a really big pike.

RECORD MUSKIES

Just as Fred Buller has chronicled the big pike in Europe, an American fishing journalist, Larry Ramsell, has investigated the "mammoth muskies" caught in North America. He has found accounts, backed up by photographic evidence or reliable witness reports, of twenty muskies weighing over 60lb, caught using rod and reel, in the United States. Out of these twenty fantastic fish caught between 1940 and 1964, fourteen were taken by four extraordinary anglers who devoted all their free time to the pursuit of these large fish: Louie Spray, Arthur Lawton, Ruth Lawton, his wife, and Len Hartman. The two biggest muskies caught by amateur anglers, and never officially weighed, were around 70lb: 69lb 15oz for Arthur Lawton in the St. Lawrence river in 1957, and 69lb 11oz for Louie Spray in the Chippewa Flowage in 1949. In fact after 1964, and until two years ago, no muskie over 60lb was officially recorded. This recent incident involved an angler fishing for walleye (a fish which is a cousin to the zander) who, in fall 1988, found a place in the record books. While preparing to tire a walleye of around 3lb, Ken O'Brien saw an enormous muskie beneath his boat, which proceeded to swallow his catch head first. By some miracle the 30/100e nylon line (he was not using a steel trace) kept a grip on the monster for over an hour. The "muskie pros" still wonder at this even today. In addition Ken O'Brien did not have a boathook on board, and his walleye landing net would barely have covered the head of this giant fish. Single-handed, he succeeded in pulling to the beach what turned out to be the sixth largest muskie caught by an angler in North America.

PIKE ON STATIC DEADBAIT

While the rest of the world has used mobile techniques for piking, such as lure fishing and moved deadbaits, the UK has developed static deadbaiting to such an extent that it now dominates the sport, accounting for something like 90 percent of the pike landed, and thousands of fish annually in excess of 20lbs and 30lbs.

Sea baits such as herrings, sprats, mackerel, sardines, smelt are used but also trout and, less commonly, roach and perch. Unlike zander pike seem to have a preference for sea fish, and do not need to be weaned on to them.

Frequently, pike will take deep-frozen baits before they have thawed out. Large deadbaits, such as mackerel and herring are cut into halves, when solidly frozen, and the halves used separately. Even smaller baits like big sardines or smelts are often used in halves. The aim is to get a bait that is big enough to be seen or smelt (remember, its vibrations will be zero) but which is mouthed quickly by the pike so that an immediate strike can be made on getting a run.

In order to strike quickly, so that the pike is not damaged by gut-hooking, a special hooking called a snap tackle is used. This consists of two size 6 or 8 trebles on a wire trace some 15 in long. The bottom hook is fixed and the upper hook is smoothly movable so that the wire does not kink when the hook is moved. At the top of the trace is a swivel for attachment to an upper trace. Most experienced pike anglers use an upper trace to avoid backlash of the bait on casting. The lead can be fixed or running, and the deadbait can be fished on straight ledger, or with a float set to just over the depth of the water. At the angler end the rod is placed in two rod rests, the front one having an electronic bite indicator and the rear one a drop-back indicator.

RIGHT *A superb American muskie. Very close to the European pike, this fish can reach really impressive sizes.*

and the cyprinidae in particular, have not yet spawned, cannibalism has a decimating effect on the ranks of newly hatched pike.

In a food rich environment, and when winters are not too harsh, the growth rate of pike is one of the most marked among freshwater fish in our part of the world (only the catfish outstrips it). At one year old it can easily reach the size at which anglers are officially permitted to fish it, i.e. 15 inches, though it will not even have reproduced at this stage. Thereafter it will gain two pounds, and subsequently four pounds, a year until, at the age of seven or eight, it reaches the famous "20-pounder" size so sought after by anglers. In the extensive limestone lakes of western Ireland, which benefits from the temperate climate of the Gulf Stream, this size may be reached in only six years as it is in several English waters. In less favored European waters it can be assumed that a 10-pounder is between five and six years old, and that a 20-pounder is around ten. Nevertheless a good performance, despite the fact that current legislation does not enable us to benefit from this fully, but allows the greedy to get away with eating our corn while it is still unripe.

As a very effective predator, living primarily on the flesh of other fish, the pike is not averse to eating the occasional frog or small amphibian mammals. It stalks them unnoticed, making excellent use of the camouflage nature has bestowed on it. Completely motionless, and quite invisible in its normal habitat, it lies in wait beneath a water plant or alongside a submerged tree stump until a shoal of roach, bleak or perch enters its area of operations. To identify the approach of its prey it uses its sense of sight and smell, but it is primarily the "radar" of its lateral line, together with the receptor pores in its head, which alert it not only to the direction, but also to the speed of approach of a shoal of fish. By means of very slow movements of its fins, it will then position itself, and it is only when the unwary interlopers enter its field of attack that it lunges forward, this time relying on sight, like a submarine missile. The position of its fins, dorsal, anal and caudal, all grouped closely together at the end of its elongated body, acts like the feathers at the end of a deadly arrow and makes possible the lightning propulsion that rarely misses its target. However, if its attack proves unsuccessful, the pike does not pursue its prey – unless that prey is

wounded and swims very slowly – but returns to its post and waits for a new opportunity. The angler needs to adapt his techniques to this behavior, retrieving his lures or deadbait as slowly as possible, using livebait or a similar lure, through some spot that is known to harbor a good specimen, and imitating the movements of a wounded fish struggling near the bottom or between two currents of water.

The muskie or giant North American "pike"

This fish (*Esox masquinongy*) has around fifty different popular names in the United States and Canada, many of which are simply orthographic variations: muskellonge, masquinonge, muskalonge, muskallunge, muskie, musky, etc. The name of this large pike (also referred to as the great pike) is derived from the old Canadian French word "masquallongé" (elongated mask, which no doubt refers to the duck's bill this fish has). Other people believe that the name comes instead from a distortion of two words in the language of the Cree Indians, "mas", meaning horrible or ugly, and "kinonge", meaning fish. In my own opinion, and because I find this fish such a splendid creature, I much prefer the first explanation, which serves as a reminder that the French language was one of the first spoken along the banks of the great American lakes.

The muskie is actually quite similar to the northern and European pike, at least in terms of its shape. For the same size fish, however, the head is smaller, slightly more pointed and less flattened than that of the *Esox lucius*. As far as its appearance is concerned, whereas the pike's camouflage markings are arranged along its length, and always look lighter in color than the background, in the case of the muskie this is the other way round. These markings or spots, when present, are more often in the form of a vertical array, or points of a darker color against a greenish-brown background with bronze tints.

The two characteristics to which scientists give the greatest importance for the purpose of identification are the absence of scales on the lower half of the muskie's cheek and gill cover (these scales being present in the pike), and the number of sensory pores on the lower jaw (5–6 in the pike, 7–9 in the muskie).

The muskie, or American pike, is very popular with anglers in the United States.

FLY-FISHING AND THE PIKE

One of the biggest pike ever caught by line was on the fly. Admittedly this was over two hundred years ago, at the end of the 18th century, and occurred in Scotland. The monster in question, taken from the waters of Loch Ken by John Murray, weighed 72lb according to the Scottish system of measurement, (at that time the Scottish pound was identical to the French, and was therefore equivalent to 79lb. The skull of this fish was preserved for a long time in the library of Kenmure Castle, and its dimensions were duly measured and verified by the British Museum. The fly measured a good three and a half inches and consisted of an arrangement of peacock, turkey and teal feathers, mounted on a red and black shaft. The tale goes that when John Murray, who had acted for over forty years as gamekeeper and water bailiff to the Viscount of Kenmure, brought this giant pike to his master, the latter exclaimed: "Come now, John, don't tell me you caught this one with a fly!"

But let us leave this fish, and the fly with which it is supposed to have been caught, to legend. Closer to our own time, a study of the very serious and official I.G.F.A. (International Game Fish Association) record book reveals, pike weighing 23lb, 22lb and 21lb respectively were caught on the fly on 2, 4 and 8 pound lines. Recently, on the Swedish coasts of the Baltic, some American anglers caught several 22–33lb pike on the fly. Yet French anglers always think that only a good 2lb chub, attached by means of tackle beneath a trimmer, is capable of taking a pike of over 20lb. It is true that in public waterways it has become rare, even when spinning, to catch a pike weighing at least 6lb, and the chances of a fly-fisher taking one are rather slim. However, there are still the private lakes and gravel pits, where pike often achieve an impressive size, and which are well suited to fly fishing. There are also, of course, the waters of Ireland, Britain, Holland, Sweden and Canada.

The fact is, the pike responds well to the fly, and in a number of ponds overgrown with vegetation this form of fishing is without doubt very effective, particularly in summer, and not only for catching small specimens. It should be understood, of course, that the term "fly" refers to any assemblage of feathers, fur, silk, tinsel and other synthetic materials, mounted around a hook, and intended for casting from a fly-fishing rod. It is in fact the method of casting, and not what is cast, that defines a given fishing method. The skill also lies in selecting the right fly, especially if tied by the angler.

Countless models of streamers, or fly lures, have been developed in North American, as well as in Great Britain and Scandinavia. In fact those intended for the pike are far simpler to make than those for the trout or salmon. Here there is no hackle to tie in evenly, and there are no proportions to be observed between the different parts of the fly. Moreover, since the flies are large even a vise is unnecessary: with a little practice, fingers will serve quite well. Four or five large feathers (saddle hackles from a cockerel), white or colored, simply tied together at their base around the shank of the hook, provide an excellent pike "fly." Except for personal satisfaction, one can give up making sophisticated models, since the simplest serve just as well when fishing. With regard to color, blue and white, with a hint of red or orange, have always proved satisfactory, but you can also try other colors in the spectrum.

For the line, depending on whether you are fly-fishing for pike in summer or winter, you will use a floating or intermediate line, or a fully sinking line. In either case, because of the size of the flies, use a W.F. which will carry the hook more readily than a D.T. As far as the rod is concerned, a class 9lb reservoir rod for line 7 or 8 is perfect. In summer you can use a floating line, which will enable you to cast to the middle of water plants and to cause the fly to perform its tricks in just a small amount of water. No other lure could perform in the small area of free water above the meadows of water milfoil or pondweed in which pike, both small and large, lie in wait.

The best way to proceed when fishing in a pond is to cast from a boat toward the edges. A useful tip is to lay a square of strong cloth on the landing area, opposite the boat, on which you can spread out your line in loose spirals. This will avoid tangles when it comes to the final shoot. Or use a line basket.

The fly should always be retrieved with the rod lowered, and by means of small tugs with the left hand, 4–12 inches at a time, interspersed with pauses of varying lengths, depending on the depth of the layer of free water in which it is being worked. The attack often comes like a flash of lightning as the fish leaps out of the water and you may be taken by surprise, causing you to reel in too sharply. Fortunately, nine times out of ten, an unhooked fish which has only bitten at a few feathers will renew the attack, if it has not seen you. On the second attempt, keep the rod low, and only pull line in when your left hand feels a firm, sound contact. If the fly again "slips," and escapes the teeth of the predator, it will remain in the water before the fish's nose, and it will attack once more.

This procedure may be repeated three or four times in succession. Once a 10-pounder attacked the streamer but was not properly hooked until the fifth attempt, less then 10 feet from the boat. Had the angler reeled in with the rod raised on each occasion, at the first failed attempt the fly would have leapt more than 6 feet in the air, and the pike, as cooperative as it was, would not have found it again and would have swum away having lost interest.

In fall and winter, when pike move back to the deeper water, you will need to use quite a different tactic. The fishing method will then be like that for casting blind, waiting for the fish to bite. A sinking line, Number 1, will be used in most cases because in a pond the bottom is rarely more than 10 feet in depth.

Retrieval must be all the slower when the water is cold, and a line that is too fast sinking would then be a handicap. The fly must be cast as far as possible, with the boat stationary or drifting, and must then be retrieved in stages, 12 inches at a time. If the water is rough or colored use fuller flies: these are more difficult to cast, but when they are being retrieved in deep water they "push" the water along, and the pike relies more on the sense of its lateral line than on visual stimuli. An attack at a depth of around 3–10 feet will simply produce a dragging sensation in the left hand. Since pike eject flies less quickly than trout in a reservoir, it is enough to maintain contact for a second or so before retrieving with several sharp pulls of the hand, which allows the point of the hook to secure a grip between the innumerable teeth that fill the mouth of this predator. However Kevlar and steel combinations allow tooth-proof traces to be cast when fly fishing for pike.

Flies that may be used when fishing for pike or bass.

PREVIOUS PAGES *The pike often hunts in open water. It is necessary therefore to present lures at all levels; they will often take near the surface.*

A magnificent fish known as the tiger muskie

The original area of distribution in Northern America would seem to be the region of the Great Lakes, both on the United States side and on the Canadian side (Quebec and Ontario). Some specialists distinguish three sub-species of muskie, depending on their basin of origin: the maskinonge of the Great Lakes (*Esox maskinongy maskinongy*), the maskinonge of the Ohio basin (*Esox maskinongy ohioensis*), which is found in the basin of that river and in the northern part of New York State and Quebec (in the St. Lawrence Seaway), and the maskinonge "of the north" (*Esox maskinongy immaculatus*), in Minnesota and Wisconsin. In fact these distinctions no longer really apply because, as a result of the great demand for this fish on the part of American anglers, these species have been introduced more or less everywhere in the central and north-eastern regions of the United States, as far south as Tennessee.

As with European pike, the muskie inhabits the still or gently flowing water of lakes and large rivers. They are generally associated with rich aquatic vegetation, and prefer clear water to muddy, or even cloudy, water. As with the pike in summer months, the muskie lies in wait in or alongside water plants, in the marginal, shallow stretches of lakes or rivers. In winter, when the vegetation disappears, and the surface water becomes colder, the muskie hides away in deeper water, but never seems to go deeper than 50–65 feet. Spawning takes place in spring and varies considerably depending on latitude, the parameter which determines water temperature. Thus, in the area of distribution further south, in Tennessee, it begins at the end of March or beginning of April, whereas much further north, in the St. Lawrence Seaway or in Ontario, it has scarcely begun in late May or early June. In contrast with the pike, the muskie is more nocturnal, and its eggs are shed either on the muddy bottom or on dead tree stumps and other detritus, in shallow sheltered spots. The female spawns an enormous quantity of eggs (over one hundred thousand in the case of a 20-pounder), the vast majority of which will not hatch (being suffocated beneath a layer of mud, or being swallowed up by invertebrates that inhabit the deeper layers of water and by other fish. However, "assisted" reproduction gives excellent results. American biologists are more and more frequently crossing a female muskie with male pike (*Esox lucius*), a cross that occurs naturally in certain rivers and lakes. The result is a magnificent fish with very distinct vertical stripes, hence its name the "tiger pike" or "tiger muskie." As in the case of all hybrids, the tiger pike is sterile, and grows very quickly. Whereas the muskie is a very wary, nocturnal predator, which is difficult to get to bite, the "tiger" is extremely voracious and readily takes the lures offered by anglers. Since it is also easy to breed in fish farms, it is currently the fish in greatest demand among American anglers. Above all it is used for replenishing small- and medium-sized rivers or lakes where fishing is in high demand. The current record is a fish weighing almost 55lb, caught by an angler casting in a Wisconsin lake. It would certainly be interesting to try out this hybrid in some of our own waters, and in particular in all the large tidal reservoirs which are not suitable places for pike to spawn, even though they offer phenomenal quantities of white fish: roach, bream, bleak and chub, which are hardly, if at all, exploited.

It is not easy getting the muskie to bite. This fish is very popular in the United States.

Returning to the muskie, however, and speaking of foragers, in its natural environment this fish also attacks the North American cyprinidae, as well as other species inhabiting the same waters. In addition it consumes large numbers of frogs and toads, young and not so young water-fowl and, for good measure, small mammals, including young beavers.

Of all the trans-Atlantic freshwater fish the muskie is without doubt the one that has most captured, and indeed stirred up, the imagination of anglers. Fishing stories involving the holding up of hands at arms' length, and about monster fish that "got away," broke the rod, or pulled a canoe several miles, are no longer recounted at "fishing camps" in Wisconsin, Minnesota or even Ontario. There people speak of "muskie mania", and it is a fact that, just as there are dedicated carp or salmon fishers, a great many anglers in the Middle West will not fish for anything else. It has been calculated, in all seriousness, that a regulation muskie (the legal size for catching this fish differs slightly from one state to the next, and depending on the river or lake in question, but is somewhere in the region of 2ft) is only caught once for approximately every ten thousand casts. However, just as with the Atlantic salmon, there are many anglers who, after more than ten years, have yet to catch their first one.

Using a spoon in combination with a squirrel's tail

The muskie is a big fish that nowadays reaches 55lb, and it makes a formidable opponent at the end of the line. By day it seems to feed little and, in contrast with the pike, often pursues its prey, or at least the imitations one hopes it will perceive as prey, all the way to the boat. It is not therefore a fish you catch every day, and the many stories that have grown up around it are mainly as a result of its rarity. In terms of defending itself, there can be no doubt that the big muskies, over

33lb say, thrash around with far more energy and fighting spirit than any large pike would display. The reason is obviously that, for the same size, these large fish are much younger than pike of the same weight. Even the largest specimens, once hooked, jump out of the water in acrobatic leaps, rather like tarpons, and it always makes one catch one's breath to see a long muscular trunk, over 4 feet in length, rise above the surface of the water like a Polaris torpedo. Most of the fishing techniques we use for the pike are suitable for its North American cousin. All forms of hardware, spinners and spoons can give good results. But the American anglers, in contrast to our own, have no hesitation in using really big lures which are likely to attract a big fish. A Lusox No. 3, or the large model of the Tourbillon or "Whirlwind" are merely regarded as bait for small fry in Wisconsin, and the firm Mepps, whose products are appreciated as much by dedicated muskie anglers as by our own trout fishers, sell a super-Lusox, corresponding to a size 5 or 6, combined with a squirrel's tail whose volume increases even more when in the water. With such equipment one does not, of course, catch many fish under 12 inches in length, but there is a greater likelihood of teasing out a really big one. Plugs and, of course, Rapalas in their larger sizes are also effective, especially the floating varieties. In summer the muskie will readily take surface lures which, more than any other form, seem to arouse its aggressive instincts. Deadbait, on the other hand, is seldom used. In fall and early winter, before lakes ice over, local specialist anglers use large free-rein livebait from the boat. "Suckers", a type of barbel weighing between half a pound and one pound, are the most often used fish, and they have the advantage of remaining active for several hours when allowed to swim around on a loose line beneath a float.

Two years ago, on the Chippewa Flowage, a gigantic artificial lake covering almost 25,000 acres in Wisconsin, the author had the greatest success, using a Drachko mount, on which were used golden shiners, a local form of roach, as bait. But as is always the case, unless one is an experienced angler, it is not very pleasant, or indeed easy, to cast and work a large, dead fish. And since 2–3 inch shiners were in use – whereas, in contrast with the locals who fish mostly with large lures, a number of fish were obliging enough to bite – nothing was caught over 12lb. In other words not a single fish worth keeping, even if it was a little above the regulation size.

Be careful of the pike's teeth! Use pliers or forceps to remove the hook.

PERCH

JACQUES CHAVANNE

Many inveterate hunters of predators have had a weakness for the perch which was a passion in their youth. To the perch they owe hours of sheer delight and other rare emotions that not even fishing experiences with large pike, or scores of zander (cousin of the walleye), have been able to erase from their memories. On every occasion they return to the perch with the same enthusiasm and the same eager anticipation. Moreover, from one season to the next they look forward to hunting them with an impatience that is difficult to contain.

So where does this fishing passion for the perch come from, bearing in mind its comparatively small size (a 2lb perch is considered a good specimen in most waters)? There is in no sense the prospect of an unpredictable, keen battle which a much larger fish is likely to provide.

To begin with, of course, one might think of the quality of its flesh, which is indeed delicious, smooth, firm and practically boneless. It is, in fact, one of the most enjoyed fish taken from European waters, and a species unusually able to compete with the best of edible sea fish. It was not for nothing that the ancients were pleased to call it the "partridge of the river", and in one's experience it has never been difficult to dispose of a catch of perch at the end of a particularly fruitful day's fishing! Nor can there be any doubt that the many varied methods of fishing that the angler is able to use to catch this fish are another important factor in its popularity. One encounters the whole range of experience: from the unsophisticated fishing rods of children who, with their basic hooks and floating line, baited from a small box containing a few earthworms, produce their first small perch; to the most intricate of fishing methods using the most individually designed lures produced by experienced specialists, in order to track down the largest specimens in their hiding places in deeper water. Indeed the perch can be fished using countless different techniques, which are as diversified as they are occasionally amusing and sometimes surprising.

All this is enhanced by other more subjective reasons, such as the elegance of this fish as it swims, or the pleasingly esthetic effect of its appearance, with contrasting colors from the bronze and green on its back, with dark vertical bands, to the golden-yellow on its sides and the orange-red of its lower fins. But it is, above all, its behavior as a gregarious hunter that

The smallest of the predators and the most aggressive; the perch is also the most handsome.

explains the popularity of the perch with the great majority of freshwater anglers. It leads to the suicidal habits of these small predators which, on some days, will attack bait of all kinds as though they were mad, enabling the angler to fill his baskets to overflowing, and, at the same time, giving him excellent sport.

Anglers will get a true appreciation of this hunting behavior when they have an opportunity to see the spectacular hunting rituals for which the perch is well known at certain times of the year. In well stocked, large expanses of water, the surface of the water literally bubbles over scores, if not hundreds, of square yards of its expanse, with the ceaseless noise of perch striking. This highlights two of its very strong instincts: that of being a gregarious fish, and that of being a predator, which explains the intense competition that prevails among them at such times. This predatory frenzy reaches the point where the fish lose all sense of natural suspicion and will jump at anything that moves! Faced with such a spectacle it is difficult to resist taking part in sharing the spoils!

It must be noted, however, that this type of behavior

PREVIOUS PAGES *Very large perch live in small groups of just a few members.*

is primarily a trait of medium-sized fish, since the truly big perch adopt behavior patterns of the lone hunter.

Another interesting feature of the perch, and not the least from the angler's point of view, is that one can expect to fish for it successfully at any time of the year, even in the middle of winter when the waters freeze over. The best proof of this comes from anglers in the northern regions who fish for perch with a success rate that has now become commonplace, by lowering their lines through holes cut in the ice. Not being able to practice this technique in France, because it is unlawful, anglers have had fruitful sessions too often, in waters that were partly iced over, to have been left in no doubt that the perch feeds all year long. But this does not necessarily mean it will take the hook at any given time or in any given season!

It is far too capricious and unpredictable by nature, in fact, for one to be able to know in advance exactly how hungry or aggressive it is going to be: between one day and the next it can pass from the most unrestrained, frantic feeding to complete apathy, without anything appearing to have changed in the fishing conditions. But there is no need to lament this uncertainty, since it is part of the pleasure that comes from fishing for this species: there can be nothing more exciting than dis-

FISHING EQUIPMENT AND TACKLE

THE ROD: Though a simple jointed or telescopic rod may be used in certain situations, a rod with rings, of the type used for trout fishing, with a semiflexible tip, is nevertheless preferable, because of the advantages it offers: the possibility of lengthening or shortening the line to suit requirements, the possibility of casting, and security when landing a big catch. A 13ft rod may be used anywhere. It should be noted that, depending on conditions, two options may be considered: either an internal thread model, when the banks are overgrown with vegetation, or a model designed for British-style fishing when a lot of long-distance casting is called for. The rod must be fitted with a small fixed-spool reel which has a very sensitive clutch.

THE LINE: The choice of diameter, and thus of strength, depends wholly on the clarity of the water, on the presence of any submerged obstacles, and on the size of the fish likely to be caught. For the main

body of the line this can range from 14-20/100e, and for the tip 12-16/100e, and even less when the water is rich in pike.

THE TACKLE: Though a wide range of tackle may be used under certain conditions, it is the floating line which offers the most likelihood of success. The leaded float mount must be chosen for maximum lightness, bearing in mind the fishing depth and the distance to be reached. If a small fixed float is sufficient under the easiest of conditions (not particularly deep water and clear banks), the slider float will offer greater advantages. The shot, consisting of a series of small spherical pieces of lead pinched on the line at regular intervals, to enable the mayfly bug to sink slowly in the water, provides the float with the correct balance, but not to an excessive extent since perch are not particularly fussy on this score. The leader, around 8 inches in length, is fitted with a fine iron hook, No. 14 or 16.

covering, by chance, one of those furious hunting sessions and taking advantage of it, even if only for half an hour. It is the experience of such unforgettable moments that leaves the angler in a flurry of emotions, all the more uplifting because they are purely a matter of chance.

For all these reasons, then, and for many others, the angler can look forward to perch fishing all year long. But this requires a knowledge of the factors that can trigger its behavior patterns, and of all the corresponding fishing techniques, a new method being required for each different season.

All the following fishing methods have in common the fact that they enable the angler to fish actively for perch. This is essential with a gregarious, unpredictable fish that must often be tracked for a considerable time before finding a group of them intent on feeding; especially if one is aware of its surprising capacity for moving around at all levels and depths between the surface and the bottom of the water (which in some areas may reach a depth of 65 to 100 feet!).

Trolling and jigging: interesting warming methods for winter fishing

Fishing for perch first entails finding it! The fact that at certain times it betrays its presence by its noisy hunting

TROLLING BAIT

The perch will usually take any bait it can get its mouth around. But only some of these can be attached securely enough to the hook to withstand the effect of the fishing technique used.
These are:

-   earthworms: the lobworm, the redworm and the river-bank worm – these are used on a No. 8-12 hook;
-   small livebait and in particular the minnow, highly resilient and a great favorite of the perch; used on a No. 8 or 10 hook;
-   carides, or small freshwater shrimp (not to be confused with gammarid), $1-1^{1}/_{2}$ inches in length, which are gathered from the lower currents of coastal rivers using a shrimping net;
-   all aquatic larvae, such as caddis-worm, caddis-bait and similar varieties, which are gathered from fast-flowing streams.

THE FISHING METHOD

After baiting the hook, allow the line to sink vertically until it touches the bottom. Engage the reel's pick-up, and reduce the line between the tip and the surface to around 3 feet. Then carefully probe the immediate area, raising the rod around 12 inches, each time moving the line sideways.

It is a good idea, initially, to insert lengthy pauses on the bottom so that the bait has time to produce its own natural enticing effect. Then, if there is no response, intensify its action by imparting more marked saw-tooth movements to the tip of the rod.

When you feel the characteristic tug of a fish taking the bait, lower the rod slightly to give the perch all the time it needs to swallow its prey, especially if the bait is large, before re-establishing contact and striking with a small flick of the wrist.

habits, thereby providing an immediate solution to the problem, makes no difference in general in this respect. It is therefore necessary to use minimal, light equipment, relying on just one rod which is kept in the hand all the time so as to facilitate movement.

Provided, of course, that any legal constraints are observed when fishing in public waters, the trolling technique is likely to provide the angler with perch (and several other species!) throughout the year, but it is in winter, more than at any other time, that this proves one of the most effective methods. During this cold period the perch are rather inactive, and the dangled bait technique, relying on three principles of attraction that have an accumulative effect, works wonders in "rousing" otherwise apathetic fish. The principle consists of dangling livebait (an earthworm, maggot, small fry, etc.) in front of the fish's nose. The natural attraction that an appetizing prey, jiggling on a hook, has for the perch is reinforced by two other methods of exciting the fish. Firstly the bait is animated vertically by moving the rod up and down, or by allowing it to sink to the bottom in each place tried (jigging). It is well known that the perch is sensitive to this type of movement which makes the bait appear more lively, and that it arouses the fish's curiosity and heightens its hunting instinct (it seems that the bait is trying to escape).

Finally, one attaches a shiny lead shot to the line. This acts as a lure or, to be more exact, as an "eye-catching" device (or teaser to serious anglers).

The perch approach their prey and watch it a moment before attacking it.

END-TACKLE USING TWO HOOKS

It is first necessary to find out whether there are any general laws preventing the use of two hooks on a line. However the large lakes where this fishing method is most regularly practiced are often subject to special regulations permitting the use of three to five lures: you are therefore strongly advised to make inquiries locally before using any form of end-tackle involving the use of two hooks! There are, of course, no such restrictions of this nature in private waters.

USING TACKLE WITH LEAD SHOT AT END (PATERNOSTERING): The main line is made from 5 to 6 feet of 26 or 28/100e nylon, to which are attached small droppers 2–3 inches long in 24 or 26/100e nylon. A pyramid-shaped lead is fixed to a swivel hook at the end of the line. This makes it possible to cast over long distances, but it needs to be moved about a considerable amount if it is to remain active, which may be a nuisance on certain days. It may, on the other hand, be allowed to drift at some depth, being kept in motion where two bodies of water meet, or near the bottom when the perch are not hunting at the surface.

BULDO TACKLE: The buldo, or bubble float, used two-thirds full, serves a dual function; it facilitates casting and, when retrieving, causes splashes similar to those produced by hunting perch, which has the effect of encouraging fish that may not otherwise be eager to feed. In addition, by keeping the line at the surface, it makes it possible to retrieve very slowly, in very short steps, and on certain difficult days this may be the only thing that will get perch to attack. On the other hand it is a little more delicate when it comes to casting, and is unable to perform very long casts.

All perch anglers have had occasion to find out for themselves that a simple lead shot, scratched with the blade of a knife, seems to attract fish at a greater distance than lead with a dull surface. It is with a view to taking advantage of this particular behavior pattern in perch that special leads, covered with nickel, and thus retaining their shine, are now available.

Above all explore the deep places

It is helpful to remember, however, that in public waters the use of shiny leads and small fry may be prohibited during the close season for pike. But, unless there is some local restriction, there is nothing to prevent the

The so-called "rainbow perch" is not in fact a perch at all, but a different species called a pumpkinseed (Lepomis gibbosus).

FINDING AND STORING SMALL FRY

Because these minute fish are very fragile, and need a lot of oxygen, it is essential to handle them with care and store them in good conditions.

They may be gathered either using a fine line with a barbless No. 24 hook, baited with a tiny maggot, or much more quickly, but only in enclosed, private waters, using a large landing net or small fine-meshed dipping net. When shoals of small fry are readily visible, you can take advantage of this and build up your stock of bait.

To keep them for a few weeks, the ideal arrangement is a fish-well in which they can be kept half submerged in the cool, clean water of a stream. Failing this, they may be kept for some time in a large tank equipped with effective aerators, placed in a cool place, a cellar for instance.

For transporting them on fishing trips, the quantity of small fry required (not always easy to gauge) must be placed in a large bucket in which the water is frequently replaced or, better still, fitted with a small battery operated aerator. Whitebait, small fish which are only 2 inches long when fully grown, are ideally suited to fishing for perch.

WHEN SMALL FRY ARE NOT AVAILABLE

Even though small fry are the ideal bait for perch, you may not be able to obtain any small fish or not in sufficient quantity (this often occurs on days when the perch are really active!). Here are a few alternative forms of bait for when you run short.

EARTHWORMS: Easy to gather and in abundant supply almost everywhere; some anglers say they need only be kept in damp moss for a few days to make them more resilient; but this author finds they are best kept just in damp, peaty soil. They need to be moved around more than is the case with small fry.

DRAGONFLY LARVAE: These can be gathered by sifting through bunches of water plants along the bank (which you subsequently replace as carefully as possible) in which the larvae are held captive. Attach to the hook as you would a mayfly larva, using a No. 14 or 16 hook, but reserve this for floating tackle.

CRAYFISH: The small crayfish is a well-known bait for large perch. It is gathered either using small pots, where this practice is permitted, or by lifting stones in running water and lakes known to contain this creature. Store in a livebait bucket and use on a No. 4 or 6 hook. Best used on retrieving tackle.

angler using matt leads and any form of bait.

In the cold season, the main difficulty is that of finding the perch, since they only rarely betray their presence by surface activity. On warm, sunny days, on the other hand, it is not unusual to observe a few small shoals of fry that have escaped the major forays during the fall, which entitles the angler to expect the likely presence of perch, urging him to scour the nearby stretch of water. If there is no visible sign, he must continue his search in the deepest places (sometimes as deep as 65 to 100 feet in large lakes), but that is no handicap for this technique, provided that leads of an appropriate weight are selected.

It is clear that, for large expanses of water, the use of a boat is essential for reaching the best places and for fishing them with a vertical line. This is the way it should be done, especially if these areas are strewn with the submerged tree stumps so favored by the perch. But even if it is the deep areas that should be fished as a first priority in open water, paying particular attention to the eddies that form behind obstacles lying across the current, one can still expect good results fishing from the bank. The use of this technique, which is simple and entertaining, often has its surprises, because on occasions zander and pike (and not only small ones!) may also be caught, particularly when fishing using small fry, which is why one should use a fairly strong rod. When one has the chance to fish in clear water, as is often the case in winter in certain waters, one should observe the way perch react: to begin with they are perfectly still at the bottom when one starts to jig. Initially the fish seem completely uninterested in the shiny lead which, because of its uncoordinated movements, sends out reflected rays of light. Then, little by little, they turn as a shoal in its direction; their fins begin to quiver.

Lift the line gently, but firmly

They then start to move purposefully, the larger specimens in the lead, all their fins on the alert, as they approach this object that has at last aroused their curiosity (or whatever other instinct may be involved), and follow it, their noses almost glued to it as it rises and falls with an animated rhythm. Finally, this little game awakes their sense of rivalry, and the moment comes when one of the perch, which was slightly behind those in the lead, darts forward and swallows the bait.

The trick then is to allow this first catch to splash around a little on the spot (but not for too long, otherwise there is the risk of the fish escaping from the hook!), which has the effect of exciting the rest of its group. It is not uncommon, when using a line with two hooks, to feel the light tugging sensation caused by another fish clamping its jaws around the other piece of bait! It is then time to bring in the line without delay, but as gently as possible.

In all cases it is necessary to remove the caught fish quickly, re-bait the line and allow it drop again, in order to take advantage of the excitement that has just been created among the group of perch.

When fishing in very deep water, it often happens that after two or three catches, the caught fish cause the rest of the group to rise with them in the water, though still deep enough for the angler to be unaware of this change. It is then necessary to avoid lowering the line straight away to the same depth as before, but to brake its descent and work it every 18 inches or so until the fish are found at their new depth.

Whether fishing from the bank, or from a boat (though one keeps warmer by walking up and down on the bank), this stalking of the perch in winter is not without its charm. Indeed many would admit to having always experienced a childlike pleasure at the water's edge, with a light rod in hand, a rucksack on the back, and protected by warm clothing, on those cold, yet beautiful, winter days when the pale sun struggles in vain to provide some warmth. To be part of this universe turned to stone by the frost, which is only hostile to those who avoid the countryside in winter, gives a really pleasant feeling of serenity and a oneness with the surroundings.

A NON-SNAGGING HOOK

Since the best places for perch are where there are plenty of submerged obstacles, it is always tempting to trail a small fry, but snagged hooks and broken end-tackle occur with discouraging frequency. The solution to this is to protect the point of the hook with a small piece of 15-20/100e piano wire, shaped like a wing sheath and attached to the shank. This method is also suitable for fishing among water plants.

When the breeding season comes

There are some winter days, however, when even the most enticing prey, presented on the lightest and finest of lines, and moved up and down in an irresistible way, leaves the perch quite indifferent. Plunged into a state of semihibernation, they then give the impression that they have deserted the lake or river altogether. On such days, an obstinate search may reward the angler with a few small perch, but this will not give any real sense of achievement and it is better under those circumstances to turn to some other predator and be done with it, returning at once, of course, if a perch is seen following a large pike spoon, or a deadbait intended for zander, without attacking it.

From the end of February, however, the perch one is able to catch using trolling or jigging methods are becoming harder to find and unimpressive in size. Their abdomens inflated with eggs, the perch now pass through a period of reduced predatory activity; they feed only on small grubs gleaned from the bottom, and move closer toward the edges and shallows where they will eventually spawn. By now the birds are singing at dawn, and the magpies are collecting twigs to make their nests: spring has come, and it is time to move on to another type of fishing.

The larva of the mayfly: a popular bait in spring

This creature is the aquatic larva of the large ephemera, the famous mayfly, well known to anglers who fish for trout on the fly. It is also known by other popular names in various regions.

This larva is the queen of baits for the perch, especially at the end of winter and in early spring, when it reaches its maximum point of development before it becomes a fully-fledged insect. It is also at this time that perch, weighed down by ripe ovarian sacs, gather together near the banks where they are to stick their long ribbons of eggs to the submerged vegetation. This larva then becomes the vital tool for seeking out the inactive fish.

Each year, however, one finds that even though many anglers have heard about this grub, few of them have yet actually used it for fishing. It comes in the form of a long larva, beige in color, with brown and russet marks. Its body is in three parts: a fairly visible head with jaws and antennae, a thorax from which project three pairs of legs, with two small sacs on top containing the future wings of the insect, and finally an abdomen formed from segments which are readily distinguished by three caudal hairs (which fly-fishers refer to as tail hairs).

It lives in the sandy/limestone layers at the bottom of certain rivers which are not polluted, and have sufficient oxygen. It may also be found in small streams where one may observe the hatching of mayflies, which in fact takes place, more often than not, in the first two weeks of June! Its aquatic life lasts two years, that is why it is always found in two sizes, but it is only the older version that is of interest, measuring between $3/4$ to 1 inch in length.

Far from being a chore, the gathering of these larvae is in fact one of the highlights of fishing for perch: uncovering a nest of these little creatures in a hollow, discovering the best areas, paddling along the bottom of a stream in order to filter out the sandy gravel and carefully pick out the larvae one by one and place them on a bed of damp moss. These are all tasks of which one never tires, and which enable one to anticipate the pleasure of stalking perch.

The effectiveness of this little creature is due to its great vitality in the water, where it quivers and wriggles in the most admirable fashion, just as it is required to, when attached lightly to a small, fine-iron hook. It should be mentioned, in passing, that it is not just a highly valuable bait when fishing for perch: a number of other species of fish also take an interest in it, even if they are not particularly large ones. It is common to catch roach, rudd, bream or tench; or even to have an epic struggle with fine specimens of carp. Moreover, in gravel-pits, a day of fishing never passes without larvae being attacked by pike of all sizes, up to fourteen times in one morning for one angler. And these are not only young specimens, as vouchsafed by a fine fish which, some years ago, put up a real fight for nearly ten minutes before giving a twist of the head much stronger than its previous attempts. Another angler caught it again on livebait, a week later, in exactly the same spot, with the nymph end-tackle still hanging from the corner of its mouth. Its weight? A little over 12lb!

FOLLOWING PAGES *A small plug is often excellent for very large perch.*

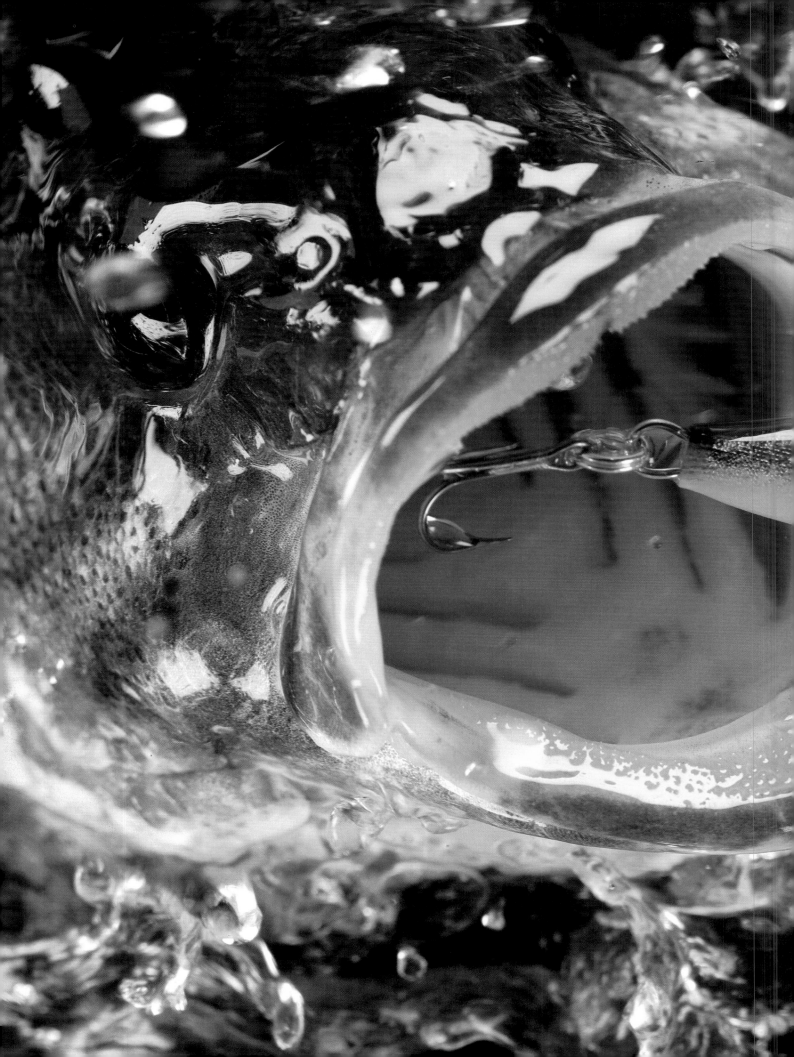

Make a systematic search of good places

Though it is possible to find significant concentrations in certain particularly favorable areas, the distribution of this fish along banks is usually in small groups. It should be noted, however, that contrary to what one would normally expect, it seems that at this time perch lose any sense of group hierarchy. Thus fish of very different sizes may be found together in the same spot, a phenomenon which would be very rare at any other time of the year. This is an important fact for an angler to be aware of, because if he catches a few unimpressive perch, this should not cause him to leave that spot too hastily: these modest initial catches may be followed by a fine batch of larger specimens.

Where should one fish? It is rather difficult to answer this question, because perch can in fact be found anywhere. Many excellent fishing experiences take place on stretches of lake and river banks which had not seemed to fulfill any of the ideal prerequisites for success. There are, of course, some general guidelines: "Show preference for banks where the perch is likely to find support for attaching its long ribbons of gelatinous eggs: young water plants, submerged tree stumps,

GATHERING BAIT

Small bait is found by sieving the surface layers of alluvium, vegetable debris and, above all, sand and gravel from rivers with fast-running, clean water. These deposits are more prevalent near the banks, but are also to be found wherever the current is slowed down, at bends, behind obstacles that create eddies, and in the lee of waterfalls.

Even where one observes the hatching of mayflies, the larvae and bugs are not evenly distributed along the course of the water.

There are some spots where, for two or three fishing trips, you can gather plenty in less than half an hour, and other spots where you have to work hard for a meager reward. You should not hesitate therefore in making a number of exploratory searches in order to find a rich "vein."

For the first attempts it is quite possible to use an old basin with holes made in it for attaching to the end of a stick, and a sieve fashioned from a few pieces of wood and a square of fine mesh. Later, however, if you get a taste for this type of fishing, you will soon want something a little more practical, i.e. a mason's sieve with a .10–.15 inch mesh, and a strong dragnet in the form of a net pocket at the end of a sleeve around 5 feet long.

It must be noted that thigh-length boots or waders are absolutely essential for getting down to the bed of the water, even if it is only of modest depth.

To start gathering bait, rake off the surface of the gravel or muddy sand, and place it in the sieve. Shake vigorously in all directions, tapping the base on the surface of the water: soon all that will be left is some alluvium and the larvae you are looking for, from which you can pick out the biggest. Do not forget to return to the water those you do not want.

Any responsible angler will naturally be careful not to take more than he actually needs, since these larvae are far too precious for that.

bushes whose roots or branches are under water, etc." But apart from the fact that there are a number of exceptions to this rule, it is never easy, when the water is not particularly clear, to tell what the bottom may be like just beneath one's feet.

The angler is far better advised, at the start of the season, to devote one or two trips to carrying out a systematic search, in order to find out where the best spots are, in fact, to be found. Time spent getting to know a stretch of water is never time wasted and will be invaluable for ensuring that subsequent trips result in fast, fruitful fishing. It should also be pointed out that this type of exploration is not at all as dull an experience as one might fear, and that it is rewarding in itself.

The only real difficulty relates to large lakes, particularly reservoirs, where the search for spawning grounds poses a real problem when one considers the overall length of the banks to be examined. It is, in fact, in waters which have a modest surface area that fishing is easiest and most rewarding.

Picture yourself, then, on the bank – a light rod in your hands, a rucksack on your back, a few accessories and spares, and a box of bait, with a large bucket or keep net to carry home the catch, plus a landing net, which is more or less essential, despite the fact that it is an awkward object, even hooked to your belt, to have to carry along overgrown paths.

Unobtrusively approach a steep, stony bank and begin by sounding the depth of the water, adjusting the float so that the bait will move around near the bottom. Once this is done, bait the hook by pushing its point through the penultimate ring of the larva's abdomen, the

only secure anchorage point, which causes it least damage and gives it the greatest freedom for its characteristic movement. It is now a question of exploring the chosen spot by first lowering the line from the rod tip, right up against the bank or alongside some submerged object. Precision and a good deal of patience is essential for this, because perch will not move any significant distance to attack larvae, as one learns from experience on many occasions.

If the fish are not biting, there is no point in persisting

When the bait is in the water, wait a few moments to allow it to perform its natural movements and then, if no interest is shown in it, proceed to attract the attention of any nearby fish by lifting the bait up and down, moving the rod in various directions. Now start all over again a little further to the side, or further out, until you have explored the whole site. You are in fact fishing with small-scale livebait, even if the equipment and light mounts are more reminiscent of other fishing methods. With only slightly weighted lines it is quite possible to visualize this small creature "working" as it causes the float to quiver slightly.

As a general rule, when there are fish around, it will not take long before they bite: a slight trembling of the float indicates that a perch has taken an interest in the larva; it is then a matter of retrieving it very slowly and very smoothly.

KEEPING BAIT

There are several methods of preserving bait. Some anglers keep it in a container with a bed of sand at the bottom covered with a layer of frequently changed water: this is going to rather a lot of trouble for what are often poor results. It is far better to keep them in a wooden box containing damp moss that has been well washed to remove any impurities. Provided the moss is kept constantly damp, and the box is placed in a very cool place (a cellar, for instance), the larvae keep at least a week, if not two, in good condition.

If you do not have anywhere cool to keep them, and

without resorting to the vegetable compartment of your refrigerator, you need to wrap the box in a large sheet of wet cloth and place it in the shade, or where there is a good through draft. This same wooden box can be used for taking your bait with you on fishing trips. Bear in mind, however, that these small creatures are sensitive to cold and to excessive dryness, so the box should always be kept wet when the weather is hot, or should be protected from frost (which is often encountered in February and March), if necessary placing it under your clothing against your chest!

LURES

Anything that spins, quivers or wobbles is capable of attracting a perch to your hook, provided that it can fit into its mouth. Here is a small selection that will serve for all situations.

SPINNERS: all spinners, leaded either beneath the blade section or at the head, which are obtainable from retailers, will serve the purpose. The most often-used sizes are Nos. 1 and 2, but under certain conditions, you may want to use size No. 0 in shallow water or for surface fishing, and size Nos. 3 and 4 for deeper water and larger perch. The basic colors are silver and gold, but black can sometimes produce excellent results. It would appear that perch are very sensitive to red decorative motifs and to added parts such as woolen pompoms, flies, small plastic fish, flexible tails, etc.

SPOONS: These are excellent for exploring deep water. Choose models 1 to $2^{1}/_{2}$ inches in length, in the same strong colors as for the spinners.

SMALL PLUGS: Though these have never been used to any great extent, small-sized plugs may prove very effective with large perch. Choose models of 1 to $2^{3}/_{4}$ inches in length.

FLEXIBLE LURES: These lures, which came out some ten years ago, have really caused a revival in fishing methods involving casting, thanks to their effectiveness, their ease of use, their low cost and their ability to move through submerged tree stumps without getting snagged. All perch fishers should arm themselves with a wide selection. Opt for models with comet shaped plaited tails, in sizes 1 to $2^{3}/_{4}$ or 3 inches in length. The colors that seem to give the best results are yellow, red and white, but all other colorings may prove effective at one time or another. They are used in conjunction with leaded heads of proportional weight, or with some other arrangement (deadbait tackle, anti-snag tackle, etc.), depending on circumstances.

The devices designed by anglers to attract fish combine a number of different effects: spinning paddles, flexible lures, etc.

Wait a moment to ensure the fish has swallowed the bait, then strike with a small flick of the wrist. Though not in top form, the finest specimens will nevertheless put up quite a struggle, which makes one appreciate the advantages of a small reel and landing net!

If the fish are just not biting, there is no point in persisting, and it is better to choose another swim. Try a spot where water is flowing in from another basin. After another quick sounding of the depth, release the reel's pick-up and allow the line to go with the current in order to explore the edge of this stretch of water: it would be surprising if there are no perch here. In fact the line has not moved more than 10 feet when the float indicates some form of contact, shakes a little and is then suddenly pulled under at an oblique angle.

A strike. But this is no small fish, and the reel whirrs in response to the forceful pulling of the fish. And then nothing! Has it slipped the hook? That could hardly be the case; it must have cut through. Quickly attach a Kevlar leader which is more resistant to the sharp teeth of pike, yet flexible enough to take perch. Attach fresh bait, cast the line once more, and again the float registers contact, this time it is being pulled sideways and away from the bank. A strike – but what a disappointment, it is only a roach the size of a hand, which is returned at once to the water! Finally some fine perch are located upstream, close to the bank, right beneath the angler's feet. As for end-tackle, this comes back an hour later, and this time the Kevlar leader holds: the fish in question is an extremely nervous 6lb pike which had almost damaged the light equipment.

Thus, by exploring in turn the vegetation near the bank, the shallows in the immediate vicinity, the obstacle strewn sides and the gently sloping banks exposed to the sun, one can test the waters, on some days with great success, on others with modest rewards, but rarely with nothing at all. Not least among the advantages of perch fishing is the almost certain knowledge you will have something to put in the creel to take home at the end of each expedition.

It must be admitted that anglers have a weakness for this traditional, environment-friendly form of fishing which requires complete harmony with biological cycles and direct, permanent contact with natural phenomena, from the gathering of larvae to use as bait, to the tracking down of perch along a great variety of banks. It does of course take some effort – and, would have to be admitted, the willingness to give up the time required – to dangle a lure from the end of a line; but it is worth it, because one never tires of this natural form of fishing!

The perch will take all sorts of larvae. If you have not had time to gather the mayfly bug, you can buy a box of other grubs from a dealer. This comes in the form of the larva of a parasitic beetle found in hives. They look like large, very fragile, white worms. The fishing method differs somewhat from that using the mayfly bug. You will need to cause it to move and jump around on the bottom. The ideal method is to fish beneath the rod tip. When a fish bites, the strike must be clean and fast, because the light bait will break up as soon as the predator seizes it, leaving nothing but the hook in the fish's mouth, which it will attempt to spit out immediately.

Keep your perch alive so that you can return to the water any you do not wish to take home with you.

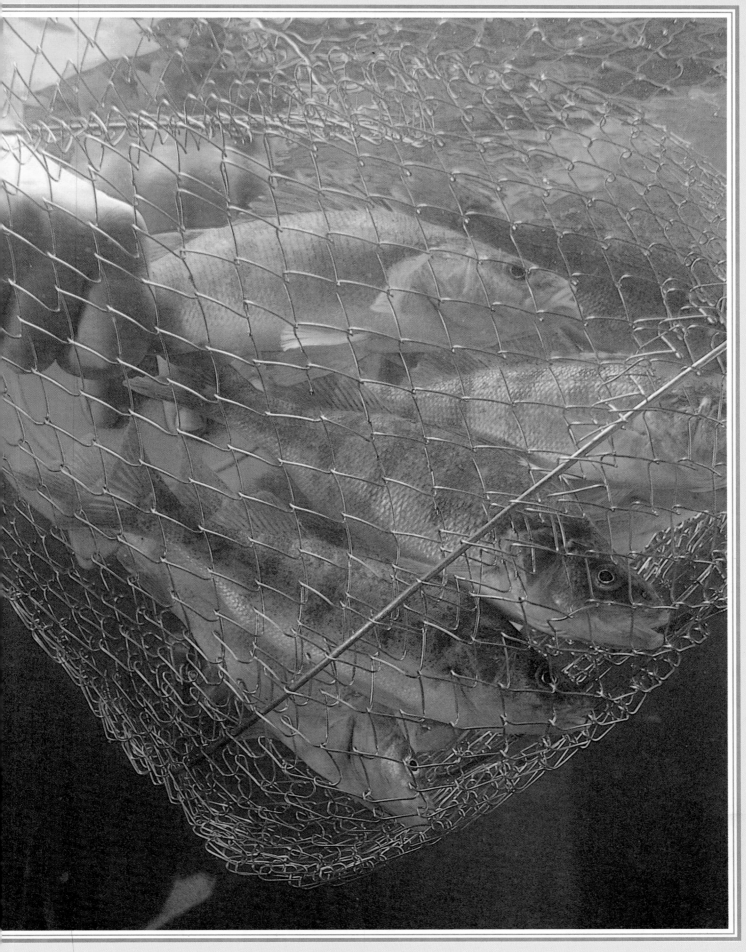

ZANDER or WALLEYE

YVAN DRACHKOVITCH

Stizostedion! Yes, you did read it correctly, but it is suggested that you read it out loud – it is even more entertaining! Tell you friends you are fishing for *Stizostedion* using deadbait, and watch their reaction! Of course, you will have guessed, or perhaps already knew, that this barbarous-sounding name is that of the zander genus, for there is not just one species of zander, but five, and the waters of Europe harbor the species known as *Stizostedion lucioperca*.

Although *lucioperca* might be translated as "pike-perch", the zander is not a cross of the pike with the perch, but a quite separate species, contrary to what you might be told at the lakeside! This mistake can be easily explained, because the sides of the European zander often have markings in the form of vertical stripes, like the perch, and its dorsal fin also resembles the fin of the latter species. In England, in addition to the term zander, this fish can also be referred to as the pike-perch.

But you do not need to be a dedicated ichthyologist; on the contrary, anglers have a poor memory for scientific names. One does, however, feel that those who passionately fish for this zander should, at least once in their angling experience, read the name of the five species that exist on our planet. Information can be obtained from a variety of interesting and informative as well as entertaining books. Ask your local librarian or bookseller – you never know, they may be anglers too!

The second group of zanders is that of the oriental family, found toward the Caspian Sea and the Black Sea. Its scientific name is *Stizostedion volgense*.

The third species of the genus is queen in North America, *Stizostedion vitreum*, the famous golden-yellow fish the Americans know as walleye.

The fourth species, *Stizostedion canadense*, or golden black, is also to be found in North America, as is the fifth, a subspecies: *Stizostedion vitreum glaucum*, or blue zander. In France it is the *lucioperca* species we have the opportunity to fish for, which gives us the largest specimens, up to 33lb, whereas the golden, black and blue zanders are small, around 2lb maximum, though this does not stop the Americans hunting for the walleye with real enthusiasm.

The zander originally came from central Europe. Following the course of canals, this species has now colonized western waters as far as northern France. The first fish were caught with rod and line in the

The walleye has an extended mouth. Notice its characteristic canines.
FOLLOWING PAGES *As with all the percidae, walleye live in groups.*

sixties. It was in 1964 that zander "fever" first became apparent. Albert Drachkovitch was without doubt the first "victim" of "acute zandritis" or "zandermania."

"Zandritis," an incurable disease

There is only one known treatment for this: deadbait fishing. But the cure takes a long time since, even after twenty-six years, despite enormous doses of this remedy, including other similar potions – pole fishing, flexible lure fishing, and other spinning techniques, fat, large worms, and so on – the patient does not seem to get better; quite the opposite in fact! The most alarming thing is that it is very contagious, even at a distance!

It would be no exaggeration to say that Albert has infected over one million anglers in France – a real disaster! There are some famous victims, such as Limouzin, Naudeau, Traissac, Imbert, Ricard and Adam; I cannot name them all because the list would be too long!

In other words, "zandritis" is incurable, somewhat similar to "salmonitis." Beware, because it seems that two new strains have arrived and are wreaking havoc among anglers: "carpitis," already widespread, and more recently "black bassitis," which came from Spain and Morocco! Nor should we forget "catfishitis" which seems to be gaining ground and is expected to have a fine future!

But why should one become addicted to zander and walleye fishing? This is a question that anglers who have not yet succumbed to the virus ask from time to time as they watch anglers travel hundreds of miles to catch a handful of specimens – and sometimes even to come back empty handed!

The zander is a mysterious, fantastic fish. One needs to be very observant to find zander on the hunt, because as a rule they are very discreet and fast moving, feeding on small fry which make very little noise as they jump, whereas the pike often hunts fish of a respectable size, which are far easier to see when they jump out of the water. On the other hand, zander do hunt in packs, like wolves, skirting the banks where shoals of small fish are to be found; then they do make a lot of noise, but it does not last for long. The zander, being a predator, requires that we hunt it, and that is why it can become a consuming

The Canadian gold is similar to the European zandèr. Its only difference is the color of its yellowish scales and smaller size.

passion. It must be left for you to guess why on one day it will feed in 10 feet of water, and the next day at a depth of 65 feet, an experience all have had from time to time in lakes and ponds! There are cycles, of course, and certain habits to watch out for – the type of places they prefer, but even if you find this in a spot you often visit, everything else may be called into question. Is the zander fisherman a cerebral angler, or does he fish relying on his instincts?

Fishing by winners and fighters, not by the lazy

He may be both. Some anglers will succeed because they are very methodical, have a good memory, and are observant. Others because they have the instinct of the natural hunter, they have a flair for it, a sixth sense; the exceptionally gifted have both!

A passion remains alive and long-lasting provided it does not become too familiar. Zander and walleye fishing is exciting because it is full of the unexpected, bitter disappointments and great joys. No one type of fishing is like any other, and there is no sense of monotony.

We mean here anglers who are fighters and winners, not the lazy or those who cannot be bothered; it is for anglers who are prepared to make their deadbait work for them, because ledgering is more suited to dreamers and to those who like to relax.

It would have to be admitted, in all humility, that in general one is able to fish fruitfully for zander for three or four hours, but not much longer! However, there are always those able to engage in this activity for eight to ten hours at a time.

The mobile deadbait one works with is in fact a camera that lacks any pictures, but relies on the sense of feeling, and depending on what one feels in the hand working the fish, via the rod, it is possible to visualize what is going on at the bottom of the water. For this, however, you need great concentration. The fishing equipment is also of great importance. Your rod and line are the components of your camera. They must send messages to your hand about everything that is going on under the water. With practice, and a lot of concentration, your hand will be able to "see" the bottom. It will "distinguish" a rock, a branch, the sandy or pebbly

The walleye seldom responds to metallic lures, though a shiny disk may attract it to the bait.

bottom, and the bite of a small fish or the nibble of a large fish; but do not think this is easy. However, the most gifted do in fact acquire a considerable skill.

Just a few months ago Albert had a call from some friends in the south: "Come at once, they're really biting!" It took little time to throw equipment into the car but it was already too late. "They" were no longer biting with the same frenzy.

However, these zander enthusiasts were not discouraged and immediately set their minds to technical and tactical fishing! An angler in one boat suddenly struck and when asked "Have you got one?" replied "No, but there's one down there!"

In those few words he had summed up all the subtlety that accompanies zander fishing using controlled mobile deadbait.

Because it is true, in fact, the zander does have an uncanny "presence", and with experience one is able to sense it.

On another occasion with Albert Drachkovitch the fishing was proving difficult and he suddenly said: "There's one following me – he's wearing his slippers and thinks I haven't noticed him! There he is, look!" He gave a sudden strike, and the zander was caught. Albert explained later that he had felt the predator nuzzling his deadbait, like a cat playing with a mouse it has killed! The zander was caught with the hook through its lower jaw.

When the zander is in a feeding mood, it attacks the bait more openly, cleanly and violently. Then it is like a dog biting at one's trouser legs! But when the zander or walleye only wants to nibble, one really has to "sharpen one's senses" if one is to notice its gentler attacks or hesitant approaches.

One speaks about the zander or walleye playing with deadbait, nuzzling it with its nose, but there is also the subtle approach to biting, usually exhibited by the larger specimens. They bear down on the deadbait as if to smother it! This produces a heavy dragging sensation which is different both from a fish taking the hook in the normal way, and from coming up against some obstacle in the water. It is then necessary to strike quickly, and the result is the fish caught beneath the lower jaw, or by a side fin!

Only when using a very fluorescent line is it possible to see this attack as the deadbait sinks to the bottom. You cast, your fish sinks, and suddenly "snap," a slight stopping sensation on the line, hardly perceptible. One must strike quickly and firmly!

The bait may be attacked even as it sinks

But that is not all. This accursed fish gives the impression that it is playing with your line! It has been experienced a number of times. At lake La Gruyère in Switzerland, with a wild storm heralding its coming with thunder and lightning, the anglers were fishing around a submerged tree. Albert had just lost his hook on the bottom. About to weigh anchor to go and recover his end-tackle when the lightning struck, Albert said: "We'd better lower our rods to be on the safe side. We can change hooks when the worst of the storm is past." They waited stoically, under the deluge of rain, when suddenly Albert said: "Look at my line!" It was moving to the left at quite a pace! He immediately picked up the rod and struck, after which he successfully landed a fine 6lb fish.

THE BOAT

Not everyone can afford a boat; it represents quite an investment. But when it comes to fishing for predators it is invaluable, because it is the only way of reaching fish that are tucked away in their hiding places along the bank. It also makes unhooking your catch easier. Owning a boat means having somewhere to keep it, a trailer to carry it, and a suitable position from which to launch it. A boat of around 10–12 feet in length is quite adequate for two anglers to share, but no more than that.

A 4-6 CV motor will do. The famous collapsible boat Albert discovered in 1975 has stood the test well, and it must be said that it is ideal for zander fishing which often requires dashing from one place to another! Easy to store and to transport, it can be launched by one person. It is indispensable. It is a favorite with town dwellers. This boat also has the advantage of being stable and unsinkable.

Other similar experiences have been had since then; it has often happened that, while having a picnic at the river or lakeside, the deadbaits have been thrown in and allowed to sink to the bottom. This has proved successful on a number of occasions, and pike are not the last to respond to this method, because this is in fact the method used in England for catching big predators. Indeed, in the UK the static deadbait is the preferred and more successful technique.

The zander must also have an innate self-preservation instinct. One often hears anglers say that this fish is becoming rarer in their area. What they fail to realize is that they are always fishing in the same place because that is where they have enjoyed successful fishing before, using the same method.

Drifting with a floating Rapala

The bridge over the Loire in Nevers has always had a good reputation (it was there in fact that Albert caught his first zander in 1964, a fine 14lb specimen). But as the years have gone by, the fish caught there have become smaller and less frequent. Then the flexible lures were brought out, and fishing improved. After a while, however, the zander became rarer.

Albert had been fishing in lake La Gruyère for seven years, in the Mimizan lake in Landes, in the Aiguizon reservoir, and in a thousand other places renowned for zander. In all these locations there were periods of plenty followed by periods of lean pickings, which were in turn followed by fruitful periods as new methods were introduced! At lake La Gruyère, for instance, the big zander stopped taking bait on conventional methods where the water was 10 to 20 feet deep. But things suddenly changed when anglers began fishing with livebait where the water was 65 to 100 feet deep!

A friend confided that, after repeated unsuccessful attempts at a large lake, he decided one day to drift with a floating Rapala in tow and once again filled a couple of baskets!

All this might lead one to think that, when it is too disturbed or worried, the zander moves or changes its feeding habits. Perhaps it has the same sense of self-preservation as the crow.

One is convinced that many animals change their habits from one generation to the next. In the country today, it is rare for a hen to be run over by a car; they keep to the edges. It is only the hedgehogs that seem

not to have understood – or it is greed that leads them to destruction, because a lot of different insects are to be found on the road. This is getting away from zander, but there are some comparisons to be made.

A change in the water quality can also alter everything. The best example is that of the Seine where Albert had some incredible fishing sessions in the middle of Paris (in 1982 on the Pont de Neuilly, with Michel Nandeau, 763lb!). Now that pollution has been reduced, and the water has become clearer, the zander is disappearing! There are two reasons: firstly it feeds on waste, and secondly it is like a vulture! Anglers will assure you that there are certain gravel-pits of limpid water, which are full of zander you just cannot catch in the daytime and in fine weather!

Moreover we all know that the best days for zander fishing are when it is dull; when the sky is gray and uniform, that is usually an excellent time to go fishing.

In the Danube delta, where Albert went in 1985, and again in 1987 with Henri Limouzin, the zander did not move away from the blue-green waters of the Danube, and were never caught in those stretches of the Danube where the water becomes clearer.

The local anglers did not know how to catch them

Albert had always been fascinated by the Danube delta. Despite what we were told by a good angler and fishing equipment retailer who advised us against going to the delta, the expedition was organized and the show got on the road. Soon after arrival, Albert asked where the zander were to be found. He was told that zander used to be caught, but not any longer. He was convinced the fish were still there, and in good numbers, but that the local anglers did not know how to catch them. And he was right! A guide was unnecessary. Back at the hotel the news quickly got around, and one evening, during dinner, a local fishing guide (who was conducting a group of German anglers) came to ask what method he should use and where were the fish!

Very politely he asked whether, the next morning, he could follow. He did, at a discreet distance, and was given quite a demonstration. Needless to say this angler became a great friend, and it was later discovered that

A good knowledge of the places preferred by walleye gives the angler a real advantage.

he is an excellent fisherman! In two days he took in every thing, and those poor zander in the delta took quite a thrashing from him!

On the second trip to the delta he taught everyone some of the secrets of fishing for catfish. This involved quite an exchange of methods.

Speaking of the exchange of methods, that leads on to discussion of the great family of zander anglers! It does exist, but it keeps a low profile. As with the zander itself. There is no club, association or other official body, as there is for the trout, the salmon and, more recently, the carp – except in the UK, where the Zander Anglers' Club is open to anyone.

The zander angler does not like noise or fuss. He prefers quiet contacts by telephone, something along the following lines:

"Hello, this is Henri. Have you heard they've arrived at Angers? Yes, Favry told me. One of his customers caught two big ones! Can you come down for a couple of days? Good, I'll see you then!"

When zander fishing started in France, Albert had his feelers out everywhere. And it was worth bringing any

FOLLOWING PAGES *The Canadian gold zander are recognized by their yellow scales. They are not so large in size as the European zander.*

findings to his attention, because having Albert come to some far-flung spot where zander were to be caught was also a good opportunity to watch him fish, to observe and to learn. He confessed that during one year he had devoted over two hundred and fifty days to fishing.

Henri Limouzin and Albert were the first to preach the good news about zander. Two very different "apostles," but perfect complements to one another, and both of them consumed by a passion for zander fishing.

The author never caught one of the "monsters." His largest zander was just over 16lb. It was November 1989, and he was fishing a large ditch from a small protruding ledge on the Loire. It was somewhat disappointing because it did not put up much of a fight. Perhaps it was tired!

Some of the best bags of zander have been caught against the backdrop of lake La Gruyère and also fishing in Mimizan, Biscarosse and Carcès.

Albert, despite all the time he has spent fishing for zander, has never beaten any records, since his biggest catch was no more than 20lb. There is no justice in fishing! One favorite fishing method is the use of mobile deadbait from a boat, going down the Loire or other rivers. There needs to be two of you, each with a car. You leave one of them downstream for use in the

evening when you need to get back to your starting point. A day spent like this, exploring a river, is a splendid experience. There is no monotony, and what changing scenes, mile after mile, as you sail downstream, without roads or houses, but only nature itself! Unfortunately, even in the heart of this natural setting there is always a tractor somewhere nearby with a droning engine.

The mobile deadbait method is both a simple and a complicated one at the same time. Your aim is to get the zander to think your deadbait is alive; this is the secret! While your hand needs to feel everything that is going on under water, your eye must be constantly focused on the line, the end section of which remains taught so that you can identify the bottom and any attempts to take the bait. The following procedure is suggested:

1.   Throw the fish, control its sinking by adjusting the end section of line, and wait till you "hear" it hit the bottom. The line then bows.

2.   As soon as you hear it touch the bottom, raise the rod so as to lift the fish from the bottom, and cause it to jump and continue moving around. This might seem simple, but it is not the case!

It requires great concentration and a sharp eye; this explains why some anglers are unsuccessful using controlled deadbait. Beginners are too frightened to lift the rod enough, forgetting that 100–130 feet of nylon line is heavy and elastic, and that if they do not make fairly pronounced movements the fish will hardly move at all!

The line may be retrieved in rapid bursts, but it may also be wound in slowly, with pauses and movements that will cause the fish to slide along the bottom.

For a beginner the ideal would be to practice in a swimming pool of clear water, so that it can be seen how the fish is moving at the end of the line. But it can also be done from a boat in 20 inches of clear water on a

The zander, like the American gold, will readily bite a streamer presented to them at the bottom.

pond; this too will give a good idea of one's technique.

It is best not to fish all the time with the rod vertical, but to vary the position, moving it from left to right so that the deadbait appears to be thrashing around madly on the bottom, or sick, because zander like prey that is easy to catch.

Spinning technique, the best way to catch zander

Little by little, everything becomes automatic and is performed naturally. The importance of the lead weight cannot be overestimated if one is to feel what one is doing. The greater the water depth, the stronger the wind or current, the larger the shot needs to be if it is to keep contact with the deadbait. With practice one can clearly sense the lead weight striking a stone or some other obstacle, and the line is slackened. One then re-establishes contact, gives a sharp tug, and the deadbait

is able to move over the obstacle without the hook snagging! When fishing from a boat it is necessary to move to a position vertically above the end of the end-tackle, and in most cases it will then come free if snagged. It is also possible to use a device for freeing snagged hooks. Some excellent devices are available on the market. From the bank it is rather more difficult to free snagged hooks, especially in ponds. In the case of river fishing there is the method used by salmon anglers at one particular torrent: they always have with them an empty plastic bottle attached to a loop of 50/100e nylon which is fastened to a split ring. They pass their line through the ring and allow the bottle to slide along the line by the force of the current. When the bottle passes the end-tackle, all that is usually required is a sharp tug on the rod to release the hook. A small piece of wood, or other floating material, can be attached to the line in order to carry it along.

In past years the mobile deadbait method was first choice. But a retailer, who is also an excellent angler

THE BAIT SPECIES

The bleak is ideal; it is, however, fragile when on the hook, and is difficult to keep.

The roach holds better and is easy to transport. The small perch has a firm flesh, but is not as shiny as the roach. Then there are minnow, chub, dace, beaked carp, and gudgeon which are preferred because they hold well on the mount. It was once generally understood that the zander did not eat carp. However, there are accounts from anglers of zander taking small carp and in the UK they commonly do so. After all, why shouldn't they? Since they also eat crayfish. And finally a word about a type of livebait which we "almost" had in France and which "should" have replaced our own old minnow.

I am speaking of the famous American minnow, the pimephales. This is a small fish with very firm flesh like the minnow, and is the same size (a maximum of

3–4 inches). Despite the very serious, in-depth study carried out by Pierre Affre (who is an extraordinary veterinary expert and angler) and by Jean-Paul Metz (professor of hydrobiology in Luxembourg, and an eminent fish breeder), the relevant French authorities decided that this species should not be introduced to our waters.

Fishermen in Belgium, Germany, Luxembourg and Switzerland have been using the pimephales for at least six years, and this fish has never invaded rivers or caused any noticeable imbalances in nature; indeed it requires very special conditions for spawning, as a result of which fish breeders engaged on reproduction tests had to give up their research!

KEEPING LIVEBAIT

This question is primarily of importance to town dwellers who do not have a cellar or garden. In the refrigerator a small bucket or large jar will keep livebait for at least a week. An aquarium, containing well oxygenated water produced by a pump is also a good method for keeping livebait. In summer you can insulate your aquarium by encasing it in polyester.

For those lucky enough to live in the country there are many options. A large tank, measuring around 40 x 20 inches, is put in a cool place. The water level must not be more than about 1 inch (the backs of the fish must reach above the water level, causing them to keep moving and, in this way, to keep the water constantly stirred up). Allow a tap to drip into this tank from as high a position as possible. In this way you will be able to keep livebait all winter, requiring only a small amount of feeding (daphnids or small pieces of worm). If your tank is outdoors, that will be all right, but the frequent temperature changes will damage the fish; a cellar, on the other hand, will maintain a constant temperature.

To keep large quantities of livebait you need a large fish pond, a good pump to produce air bubbles, an active carbon dechlorinator and, above all, a cooling unit in the water to keep it at a low temperature. A freezer full of water, and set to its minimum setting, makes an excellent fish pond!

It is now quite easy to transport livebait, thanks to battery operated pocket aerators, or the sort that can be plugged into the cigarette lighter in your auto. One can buy current converters. Fitted to a cigarette lighter, it transforms 12 V to 220 V and is then able to power a more powerful pump than a battery-powered aerator. This is ideal for long journeys and for transporting a large quantity of livebait. It is also possible, in some place, to buy pastilles that put oxygen into the water. Note, however, that water in which livebait are kept should never be changed all at once. This can be fatal, especially when they are transferred from hot water to cold. Do it in stages. This may take longer to do, but it is worth the effort. Do not put your hands into the tank to transfer your livebait to a bucket, use a small net to avoid injuring them.

and zander enthusiast, introduced a new technique. In 1970 he only fished using a spinning method of his own style, and considered it the best method for zander, the mobile deadbait method being only for tourists!

His technique is, in fact, simple and effective. In terms of equipment he uses little: a No. 1/0 or No. 1 hook, a 20 inch leader or trace, a swivel, and above it floating olivette weighted to correspond with the force of the current. The small fish is attached to the hook through the mouth, making the point emerge through the back to hold it in place, and a rubber stopper is fixed to keep it in the right position on the hook. He then casts this a considerable distance, allows it to drift, and then gives a number of slow pulls so that the fish is trailed along the bottom, with lengthy pauses, as though it were about to die. This is a very touch-sensitive form of fishing, because as soon as he feels a fish taking the bait, he releases the reel's pick-up to enable the zander to swallow the bait and move off 6 feet or so, and then he re-engages the pick-up, retrieving the line quickly and firmly. It is a technique one can use in places which are often fished using deadbait and flexible lures. Moreover, on a recent trip to the Seine in northern France it was observed that this method is coming back into fashion.

Trotting, using livebait and floats, also has its charms. A long rod of around 11ft, floats, a stop-knot or commercially available "Stopfil" in rubber or wire, a 20 inch trace or leader, a floating olivette in a stop on a lead weight, and a single No. 4 hook. The small fish is attached by both lips.

The line is held in the left hand

One starts by casting upstream, first near the bank, and then further out. In order to give more life to the fish used as bait, check the float and then release it. If the terrain permits it, walk along, following the float, so that you can search by allowing the end-tackle to sink.

An excellent variation on this technique is trolling. From the bank you will need a long rod, some 16–19ft in length (this is now difficult to come by!). From a boat 13ft will be sufficient.

The same tackle as above, but without a float. An olivette, which may weigh up to one ounce, depending on the current, will make it possible to keep the line taut and to trail the livebait along the bottom.

As with trout fishing, the line is held in the left hand

so that it can feel the livebait working and any obstacles that may be present. Be on the look out for fish taking the bait as it sinks; this is a frequent occurrence and may be detected by a slight displacement of the end-tackle from which one must not move one's eyes!

However, one does not always have to run up and down to catch zander. There is also the tranquil technique of pole fishing. This is not really for the active person. But one day everyone will slow down a little!

The hooks used may be singles, trebles or doubles, with or without a ryder. The size will depend on the livebait used, and these will be attached through the mouth, behind the dorsal fin, and behind the anal fin.

Take a float of around 8 inches, preferably the internal slider floats, and of balsa rather than cork.

Henri Limouzin has written a whole book on fishing for zander using the fixed pole method, involving fiendish accuracy and technical skill! It appears there is an incredible choice of methods, yet someone will come along and say: "Well I do it in a different way, but catch just as many as you!"

The technique is simple: the deadbait is allowed to sink to the bottom and it then waits for a zander to pass. The largest specimens are often taken in this way.

Equipment

When it comes to fishing from the bank two different types of rod are needed, depending on the water in which one is fishing. In ponds, lakes, reservoirs, canals, the rod will be 11–14ft long, able to cast weights of $1-1\frac{1}{2}$ oz. It must be able to cast long distances, and yet do so gently, because livebait is often light and fragile (the bleak, for instance). The through action, or parabolic rod which means that the rod works from the handle to the end of the tip is preferred. This is a typically French action which has now been introduced to the US market. The stiff American rods which have almost all their action at the tip are now being increasingly replaced through action or parabolic rods. The British have always preferred these.

Let us return to the "stillwater" rod. Enormous progress has been made over the last five years. There are now extremely good telescopic rods, which are ideal

Walleye hunt in groups, and herd up small fry before attacking them.

for carrying, when mobile fishing and for packing into the trunk of your car.

When fishing the current using livebait the rod is far shorter, because this is short-distance fishing along the bank. A rod of about 8 feet is recommended because this is also ideal for fishing from a boat. In other words, a single rod for two types of fishing. Semi-stiff action: this is the general characteristic of a zander or walleye rod, because it requires both flexibility for casting, and power for holding on to a fish which has decided to take refuge in a submerged tree.

For fishing from the bank using mobile deadbaits, rod lengths of 9–10ft are necessary for long casts, and for good control over the line between the tip of the rod and the end-tackle. A 6ft rod would only fish correctly at a distance of a few yards, and the hook would snag more frequently. It is possible to buy semi-adjustable rods, which means that they may vary in length, say from 6 to 8ft or even 9ft, because they have a telescopic handle. This might seem an attractive idea, but it must be admitted that these rods have no "soul" and perform badly when it comes to transmitting information to the angler's hand, resulting in lost fish and frequently snagged hooks.

For fishing from a boat using mobile deadbaits an 8ft rod would seem perfect, and this has been adopted by nine out of ten anglers who engage in boat fishing. A shorter rod produces a sharper casting movement which can damage the bait, and also result in less sensitivity in the angler's hands: and it needs to be repeated, your rod has to tell you what is going on under the water!

The reel

This has a less significant role to play than the rod, and beginners would be advised to put more money into the rod than into the reel.

The market now offers a large choice. At least

A superb Canadian gold.

WHAT EQUIPMENT SHOULD YOU USE?

It is possible that modern industry will invent new equipment; however, it is safe to say that the rods now available are almost perfect.

When you go to your retailer, you have the choice between carbon rods or Kevlar-carbon rods, the latest arrivals, which do not make any significant improvement in terms of the action, but are perhaps better in terms of their strength.

Then you could opt for composite rods, that is to say made from carbon and other materials. Some anglers like the action of these rods which are slightly more flexible, and less jerky, than carbon, and the price is also lower.

Finally there is always glass fiber, and the quality/price ratio of these rods makes them a good choice. But the weight of these rods remains a serious handicap for a long day's fishing. They are also less sensitive than carbon rods, but when the budget is tight, they make good fishing equipment.

Whatever your circumstances, do not allow a retailer to talk you into buying whatever it is he wants to sell: if you want to use the mobile livebait, you need a fairly stiff rod, but you don't want a "cow's tail!"

Avoid buying a rod that comes with a screw-on reel attachment, because you will not be able to choose the position of the reel to suit your hand and to balance the rod as you would like to.

Good rods come fitted with movable reel seatings, which are now made from plastic, so they are more flexible and less cold than the old metal rings. One can do without reel sealings, and attach the reel using a strap cut from a tire inner-tube (15 x $\frac{1}{2}$ inch), like the straps used on surf-casting rods. It is as if the reel were welded to the rod, with excellent holding properties, and even in winter it is not cold to handle! Electrical insulating tape serves just as well.

Speaking of rubber straps, here is a good trick for separating two sections of rod that will not come apart. It is almost infallible. You need two strips of rubber, measuring 15 x $\frac{1}{2}$ inch. Wrap one strip around the end of one of the sections near the fitting, in overlapping spirals, pulling tightly as you wind; this forms a grip. Do the same on the other side of the joint. You can now pull and twist the two sections away from one another, and your hands will not slide. Numbers of rods other anglers thought were past redemption have been rescued in this fashion.

twelve big brand names are vying for the market, not counting the lesser branded ones which are at least as many in number!

The reels to use are the simple ones where the risk of things going wrong is limited. There are some reels, centre pins, where the only mechanism is a pulley and a sprocket, and this is usually sufficient!

Swiss anglers, and the people in Savoy, are fond of fishing with the "frame." What is a frame? An inhabitant of Geneva would tell you: "It is a reel from the Vaud canton." And the inhabitants of Savoy, hearing this, would dispute such a statement, stating categorically that it is a Savoy invention!

Whatever the case, all you need to do to make a frame is take an old slate writing board, as used by school children in past generations, (if the antique and trendy "by-gones" shops have not found them all), remove the slate, and there you have a wooden frame. Roll 100 yards of nylon line around this frame, and you are ready to fish. It is quite a sight watching a skillful angler using such a frame, and the results are spectacular, particularly when fishing with minnows, because retrieval produces a very jerky movement which is excellent for catching zander! Yet it is rare to see a zander angler using a frame!

The spool

Take another look at the reel, and at the qualities it needs to have for zander fishing. It must of course be light, 10–10$\frac{1}{2}$ ounces. What would be the use of a light rod if the reel were heavy? A simple mechanism will reduce the risk of mistakes. If you can get used to it, dispense with the pick-up. It will be one less mechanism to bother with. Few anglers now use the method of retrieving the line using the finger.

It is also essential to have a precise, reliable clutch mechanism which is very progressive in action, not one of those hiccuping clutches that snatch the line in fits and starts! The antireverse mechanism must be firm and silent. These need not be used at all. Why? Because in the event of a large fish taking the bait, taking the angler by surprise, and with the clutch badly adjusted out of carelessness (which does happen!), it is possible to release the reel handle, and perhaps even to unwind some of the line to prevent it snapping. Perhaps it is also because we are so used to our old reels, the clutches on which are not as reliable as on today's models!

The spool needs to be as large as possible! For years now anglers have been trying to impress on manufacturers that small spools are a real mistake. The line bulges out and kinks can occur.

It must hold 100-150 yards of 20/100e line, because it is rare, and indeed inadvisable, to fish for zander using a stronger line. This diameter is used for fishing in overgrown spots where there is a significant risk of snagged hooks.

The line

In 1978, when Henri Limouzin gave us his *Secrets of the Zander Angler*, he wrote, in connection with the line to use: "If you are able to get it (because it is not yet sold in France), you would be well advised to go for luminescent nylon line, which remains clearly visible in twilight and on overcast days ..." How things have changed in the intervening twelve years!

Line is now fluorescent and improves from one year to the next. Not to use a fluorescent nylon when fishing for predators or carp is to forfeit a significant advantage. Even if you have very good eyesight, if you use a transparent line you are bound to miss a good number of potential catches.

It has been proven that fish are no more likely to see a fluorescent line than any other sort. So why do certain anglers persist in not adopting the fluorescent line? They are depriving themselves of a real benefit, both for their fishing and for their eyes. The old ways are not always the best.

Moreover, a flexible line will cast better and will be less likely to form kinks than an inflexible line. Flexibility is one important quality, but the line must not be elastic because, if it stretches too much when being retrieved it may result in failure. It stands to reason, because a lengthening of the line will slow down retrieval. To illustrate this fact, one need only consider the anglers in Savoy who fish with dead minnow, using 30/100e or even 40/100e line, on inflexible rods as stiff as broom handles! This is not by chance. It means that when you strike it takes immediate effect, and the hooks take a firm hold.

Walleye often keep close to obstacles and piles of rocks, and this makes them difficult to find.

Swivels

Consider this heartbreaking event, brought to mind by thinking of swivels. Three men were fishing from a boat: Albert, a retailer of fishing equipment, and the author. On this day, when the fish were just not biting, pike being the quarry, it was hoped to catch a fish for the guest. Suddenly a fish took the bait, and it was on the guest's rod. A struggle ensued, and when the fish reached the boat the angler in question asked Albert to take it for him; but just as he was on the point of taking hold of it, the pike made a sudden dash and snapped the end of the line, even though its strength was 40/100e. Amazed, Albert took hold of the angler's line and tested it – it was new. He looked at the end of the line and saw that it was chipped along a $\frac{1}{4}$-inch section. He asked:

"Is your end tackle made of steel?"

"Yes, a big 20 inch one; its strength is over 17lb!"

"I can't understand where the swivel could have broken!"

"Oh, I never use them!"

It was politely explained to him, that his steel wire had cut through the nylon, and he was told what a swivel was for! I'm sure he sold more of them after such an embarrassing experience!

The quality of a swivel is important. Some will last forty years!

Fitting a deadbait

If anyone had told Alfred, twenty years ago, that fishing would make him famous, he would have thought it was a joke! He has never done anything to make this happen. People just sought him out, and it has all come about despite him! It would never have occurred to him to sell his hook mount. Yet it has become so widespread that there was a reservoir where the local fishing association posted a notice in large letters: "Fishing using a 'Dracrovitch' mount is forbidden"!

Yet they permit fishing using livebait!

Henri Limouzin has described very accurately the way in which a Drachkovich mount can be made. This is an excellent activity for winter evenings, but Albert never made too many in advance, preferring to see what there would be in the way of livebait; when necessary, making them in a panic before going to bed the night before.

There is now a number of different size mounts on the market, and No. 1 is recommended for zander.

With adjustable mounts you can vary the length of the trace to the rear treble, depending on the length of the livebait used.

STEEL TRACE, OR NOT?

When zander fishing first began, there was no question of using steel traces. It should be said that over the last ten years the quality of steel traces has changed significantly, and you can now get very fine steel wire, 25/100e, with a breaking strain of about 10 lb. This wire knots like nylon and has less spring than earlier wires. Moreover it can be easily straightened out by pulling firmly on it.

Steel traces, or the Kevlar and steel variety, are to be recommended because in most cases when zander are present there is also the risk of pike that could break the line. Pike bite easily through ordinary Kevlar which lacks a steel core.

We can now get extremely good steel wires which knot like nylon and are very flexible. They are sold in the form of traces fitted with swivels or as 10 ft coils. This latter is the best formula, because you can choose the length. It is also more economical.

The steel wire, covered with nylon is not as easy to use as the other types. Some anglers find it practical, because it is possible to make loops with splices which are heated slightly with the flame of a lighter so that the nylon fuses together.

The Kevlar came out around the late eighties. It is used to fish for predators, and more recently for carp. Its great advantage is that it behaves exactly like wire and does not therefore distort. It is also very easy to use. It does, however, need to be watched: if you catch a number of pike in succession, their teeth are likely to cut into it. There is also Kevlar wire with a steel center. This was tested in Ireland for eight days, and found to be an excellent product which was easy to use. It is a little less flexible than the Kevlar and does not distort, yet completely eliminates the danger of pike biting through the trace.

The trace may measure 8–12 inches, depending on individual preferences. It should be fairly long because, if the lure is changed quite often, a 30/100e leader will soon become shorter!

Despite their characteristic canine teeth, walleye are unable to bite through a nylon line.

When this mount came out, many anglers gave a sigh of relief, because it avoids the need for a whole range of mounts for each fish length. The first time Michel Naudeau displayed his box, or his case of hook mounts, it was very impressive. The lengths of the traces were marked in each compartment, in one-sixteenth-inch gradations, with various lead weights up to $^3/_4$ ounce.

It is essential to be able to adapt quickly to all the different waters one is likely to encounter. A lake with an average depth of 5–6 feet is fished using a quarter ounce weight. But as soon as you come across a deeper section, or if a strong wind starts to blow, you will need a heavier weight. The "Drachko" system makes this easy to do, especially if one uses the extremely useful pliers developed by an enthusiastic fisherman who also happened to be a skillful handyman impatient with what the tackle suppliers had to offer. You can find shot in $^1/_2$ ounce sizes without any difficulty, but sizes up to $^3/_4$ ounce are rarer.

Yet it cannot be imagined fishing in depths of over 50 feet without shot weighing a good $^1/_2$ ounce. If there is a current, you will need $^3/_4$ ounce. The weighting accounts for 80 percent of the success, because only a weight that is well suited to the conditions enables you to "see" the bottom.

What fish should one use on the mount? Above all others the best are live fish (which one kills with a sudden flick before attaching them to the mount). Frozen

The controlled worm is an excellent technique for catching walleye. Here, the fish is waiting.

The worm passes nearby, held near the bottom by the lead weight. The fish seizes it.

fish do not lose their attractive appearance, but they go off rather quickly. Preserved fish in cans are also useful. These are readily available and the results speak for themselves: they do catch fish. Always keep some in the car, because it provides an excellent back-up for a fishing trip decided on at the last minute, and for trips abroad when one is not sure whether livebait will be available! They now come in unbreakable sealed plastic jars. The size of these fish is about 3–4 inches. This is a good choice and they can be used to catch both average and large fish.

Natural bait

Fortunately the zander does not only respond to mobile deadbait and live fish. It will readily accept other baits. Big earthworms, which one can now obtain easily from dealers, or which one collects from the lawn with the help of an electric lamp, especially after heavy rain, are excellent baits.

The mounting of the line is quite straightforward: to fix the worm to the hook, take it by the head and push it on one of the arms of the treble in the position where it has its large protruding ring, with the head lightly passing the hook. Then, turning the worm round, press it on the other two arms of the treble.

You need to lower the tip of the rod for a moment so that it can swallow the bait. Then it is time to strike.

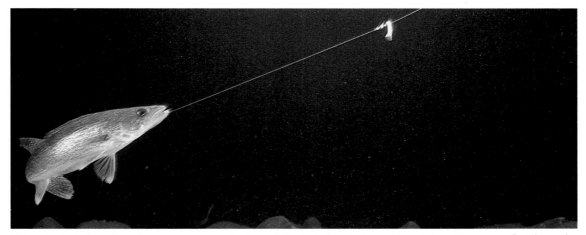

When hooked, the walleye does not put up much of a struggle. This fine specimen does not have the energy of a pike, and can be landed without difficulty.

Obviously this sort of bait needs to be cast smoothly, and it is necessary to check the line slightly when the worm reaches the surface of the water in order to prevent the shot from falling first.

A rind of fat makes an excellent form of bait to use during the close season for pike, when livebait and lures are banned.

Rind can be readily obtained from butchers' shops and delicatessens. It is easy to cut with scissors. A piece 3–4 inches long and about half an inch wide provides a good imitation of the shape of a small fish. Push two arms of a treble hook (No. 7 or 8) through one end. The same mount as for the earthworm.

Attaching the lead weight to an extension link is useful, especially when the bottom is stony. This prevents hooks being lost whenever the lead shot gets trapped between two stones.

In the case of sandy beds, the shot is mounted on a link swivel.

Flexible lures

The first sales of flexible lures were in Geneva back in 1975. However, since the mobile deadbait gave excellent results, the use of flexible bits of plastic was not fully appreciated.

A truly "fishing fanatic" friend of mine, was one of the first people to believe in the flexible lures and to give them a thorough testing, with surprising results. A number of his articles in the specialist press soon revealed that he had a large following. There is now a wide range to choose from: lures that are mounted on a hook which is lead weighted, lures that imitate a fish which are fixed to a mount and are excellent alternatives to the deadbait.

Lures for vertical jigging

Their ancestor is obviously the metal fish that were to be found in fishing tackle catalogs of 1900.

They have been popular for some time in Scandinavian countries. The excellent Stingsilla (Norway), which has been distributed in France for several years now, is one of the best.

All in all, jigging is not particularly popular in France (termed "trolling" there), "because there are risks" fishing among branches and submerged trees. But those daring enough to try are often rewarded for their effort.

Wonderful catches and excitement are guaranteed! You need to have fast reflexes, because the zander has to be snatched from its lair. For this method of fishing you would need to use a stronger line than usual: 30/100e will do the trick.

Swiss shops sell what are known as "Jukers", which are actually pieces of hexagonal silver or yellow brass, which vary in size from 1–3 inches. There are also splendid versions in mother-of-pearl, with small wings at the end which cause them to turn.

Spoons

This will be a short paragraph, because it is quite rare to catch zander using the spoon. Speaking for the author he has only caught one, using a spoon. It was at spawning time, and gave the impression it was more a question of defending her eggs, than of a feeding reflex.

So there are no "special" spoons or spinners for zander. If one has to choose, go for a spoon which can be made to work much as a mobile deadbait. Whatever is used, it is always necessary to make a spoon move about, either with the rod, or during retrieval which must be irregular in its pace.

Zander have a reputation for not responding to spinners. This is generally the case; however, the large specimens may often be taken in this way. Is this a contradiction in the behavior of this very individual fish? You can be assured, it has not yet finished springing surprises on the enthusiastic angler.

Plugs

Nor can one say that plugs hold any particular attraction for the zander. You would need to jig very expertly with this type of lure.

However you can try your luck from the bank. Choose a small plug and, instead of retrieving it in bursts, as with the mobile deadbait, turn the reel evenly. The plug, in contrast with other lures, works by itself, which is what makes it ideally suited.

The worm is an excellent bait to use for catching walleye. If you do not wish to use earthworms or black-headed worms, there are some very attractive imitations.

SALMON

MARC SOURDOT

Of all the species fished for sport the salmon is without doubt the one to which most stories are attached, and the one whose dealings, or should one say relationship, with the angler, are most characterized by unreasonable behavior. Moreover it is the most mythical and the most threatened.

As a gift from the ocean to the river, a present from the sea for those living on land, those who have not always known how to harvest the ocean's riches, the salmon is disappearing from many British, Irish, French, and other rivers. One by one, they are being abandoned by this fish of kings, or indeed king of fishes.

From its infancy, spent in the upper reaches of rivers, it retains the memory of cold waters, and this guides it, once it reaches adulthood, a living shaft of muscle, on its return journey toward its spawning ground urging it on, to its own detriment, toward the angler. One becomes a salmon fisher by association, out of curiosity, or by chance. But often it is an obsession and the cause of some grief, either to the angler himself or to those close to him. There are two categories of salmon fishers: the occasional angler and the obsessive.

The first type rarely exercises his skills on a single river which is often too deserted to give him a reasonable chance that one day he will savor the pleasure of combat. He prefers traveling and making use of the well-frequented fishing areas so ably preserved, managed and profitably operated in Ireland, Scotland and Norway. On those famous waters he has a much greater chance – though not the certainty – of measuring himself against this great fish. So each year several thousand anglers leave Europe and head for those far-off rivers. For them the salmon is only one holiday destination among many. When they return home they scarcely think about it again until the next trip.

But there is the other category, those for whom it is an obsession and who are afflicted by the condition known as "salmonitis", a form of monomaniacal neurosis which, in its worst phases, takes the worker from his factory, the rancher from his herd, the doctor from his patients, the husband from his wife, and the father from his family. For those suffering with this affliction, the disease is more reminiscent of Dante's Hell than Alice's garden. You must "abandon all hope" when you contract "salmonitis".

The obsessive French angler fishes all over France

There are two large families of salmon: the Atlantic salmon (Salmo salar) which is found mainly in British, Irish, Scandinavian and Canadian rivers, and the Pacific salmon (Sp. Oncorhynchus), which is found on the Pacific northwest coast of America.

and Navarra, throughout the season. It starts in Brittany, which is one week earlier than Allier; the close season on the Gave being a fortnight later than other rivers. And if he has the time, and can afford it, you will find him in Ireland in July, in Norway in August, and finally in Scotland in the early fall. One might wonder at the reason for this all-consuming passion which is not found elsewhere in the angling world.

The rarity of salmon may have justified its high price – though this is not the case with salmon from fish farms in Norway – but it does not help to explain the role played by wistful dreaming and the grain of folly involved in this pursuit. The "old hand" is just as excited when he catches his thousandth salmon; the pleasure never palls. When the fish bites on the thousandth occasion, the heart beats just as strongly. This encounter with salmon always has something of a first meeting about it. Even in foreign waters, where the taking of a salmon is of no statistical significance, one meets the same symptoms of the same passion. Thus my friend Audun insisted on having his retired father stand in for him for two days, rather than miss one of those splendid ascents of the salmon in our small Rogaland river in Norway, even though during the same year he had already had over one hundred salmon to his credit. Or take another angler who forgets his pain and rheumatism – even though they are real enough – as soon as he reaches the river; and should the situation

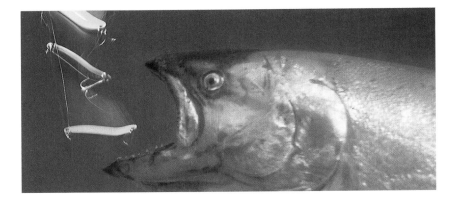

SALMON FISHING USING SPOONS

This is an early season method of fishing, when the water is cold and the water level high. You should use spoons weighing 1–1½ ounce if using a multiplier reel, attached to a direct mount. On a fixed-spool reel you may use a much lighter spoon, weighted by means of a boat or Wye lead attached 3 feet from the lure, this distance being necessary in order to avoid restricting action and the butterfly-like movements of the spoon. You should choose models which are best suited to the profile of the waters you are fishing: depth, water temperature, and the speed of the current. In fast-flowing water, these spoons will have a tapered form, whereas in calm water they will be broader and heavier.

The fishing action consists of causing the lure to move in the immediate vicinity of the fish and then, through the cold water, making it work primarily near the bottom. The line is cast three-quarters downstream, after which you must re-establish contact with the spoon and maintain this, with the rod raised, while it drifts downstream, from time to time correcting the tension of the line when fishing with a fixed spool reel, with a turn or two of the handle. In contrast with fishing for other types of predator, this is not a method that relies on animating the lure or bait, but on sustaining a fishing method. When the spoon has stopped drifting, retrieve and cast again, each time increasing the surface area being fished, taking one step downstream, or casting further out.

A fish taking the bait will make itself known by means of a sharp, violent pull, or simply by means of a check on the drifting movement. As always with salmon fishing, if in doubt, retrieve the line with all your might, lest your lure become ensnared at the bottom or on a tree stump. It is when fishing with a spoon that one experiences the greatest number of fish slipping the hook. It is assumed that, using the blade of the lure as a lever, the salmon succeeds in freeing itself. But it may also mean that it is this lure which produces the greatest number of bites.

demand it, he is quite prepared to jump from one rock to another across the foaming surface of the water.

Nor can its rarity, size and weight fully explain the fascination this fish has for the salmon enthusiast. The largest salmon caught in France, and the official record reported by the magazine *Fishing and Fish*, caught by Jean Hérault on the Allier in 1974, weighed 36.3lb. Every year in Norway a number of grand specimens weighing in excess of 50lb are caught. But it should not be forgotten that the record for the carp is just over 80lb, and that every season catfish weighing over 110lb are caught and recorded.

The way the salmon defends itself is doubtless one factor that goes a long way in explaining this strange obsession with the species, even if this varies considerably in duration and intensity, depending on how young the fish is. Its defence will be violent and obstinate, and will always be long if it has had time to rest in the pool where it is being fished. Its struggle will be shorter if it has only just arrived, tired from the distance covered or from the obstacles it has negotiated on the way. Similarly the water temperature has a direct affect on the fish's behavior and on the length of the struggle. It is between 43°–57°F that the salmon puts up the best fight. Colder or warmer water slows its activity and tempers its reactions.

There can be no doubt that the attitude of anglers in the second category is explained more by the behavior

SALMON FISHING USING THE SPINNER

This is the fishing method used at the start of the season on the Allier, and throughout the season on rivers in Brittany. Widely used abroad in several countries, the spinner has also become very popular in Ireland over the last three or four years where the "Quimperloise" model is having great success. On certain fast-flowing rivers in Norway, on the other hand, the local anglers use very large lures of the "Giant Killer" type.

On large rivers one approaches the subject in much the same way as for the spoon, using the sustained retrieve method, allowing the spoon to work on its own, after casting at right angles to the bank or slightly downstream. The weighting of the spinner, when required, will take the form of shot or of a boat lead, pinched on the head of the lure, or on the swivel. Where there is a strong current, choose a spinner with an elongated blade that turns close to the body, and a wider, more rounded, rotating blade in slower moving water.

On small rivers, with the aid of lighter equipment, you can use the famous "Quimperloise", spoons No. 2 or 3, appropriately weighted on their axis, and fitted with a white or red rubber fringe. The vibrations of this small, extremely mobile appendage no doubt add to the attractive powers of the lure. In order to limit the adverse effects of kinking and the premature wear of the line, a link swivel may be used.

The fishing action is quite similar to that used in trout fishing: you cast three-quarters upstream, and retrieve the line, causing the lure to work. It is often at the end of its line of movement that a fish will take the hook, since the change of rhythm can have the effect of triggering the aggressive instincts of the fish.

This method has nothing in common with the sustained retrieve technique. It combines the precision, delicate touch, and effort required for the effective use of this lure, which, is one of the most deadly.

of the salmon, the result of its disconcerting, unpredictable, and unusual nature. For hours on end it will shun lures, refuse the bait or flies presented, and just occasionally thank you with a mocking leap or a more discreet movement, just in case you should forget it is there and be tempted to reduce the pressure. Then, for no apparent reason, it will pounce on a Devon as it passes for the one hundredth time. And that will be reward enough. This also helps to explain the strange relationship that exists between a fish of remarkable character and a somewhat crazy angler: it is the meeting of two manifestations of harmless folly locked in a dual, whose outcome can never be guaranteed.

But whatever species one belongs to – whether the obsessive angler, or the more reasonable type – the salmon is also admired because of the way it moves, the perfection of its well defined contours, and its changing colorings: in short for its beauty.

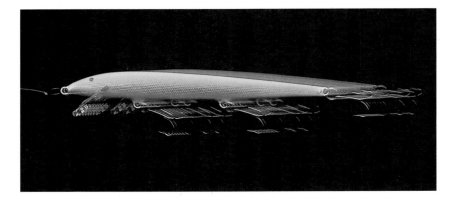

SALMON FISHING USING THE DEVON

This is the ideal lure to use on large rivers. In the first case it is metallic, and has a black and red pyjama stripe design, weighing between 1 and 1½ ounces. The traditional Scottish Devon is made from painted wood, and is weighted or unweighted depending on the waters being fished; more recently they have been made from synthetic fibers. This lure makes it possible to explore the whole surface layer of water if you are using the wooden Devon, and all the way down to the bottom if using the heavy Devons made for the deeper rivers. Ideally it should be used in deep, regular currents, where it can fish alone without necessary movement, apart from the alternating tugs and releases, accelerated movements and enticing stops in areas known to be inhabited by salmon. Its rotation and very fast oscillation make it a lure with a wide effective radius which can often cause a fish to bite.

It is used in moderate, or slightly warmed waters, although some "old hands" use this lure exclusively from the start of the season through to the end.

Though easy to use, it requires certain precautions if one is to avoid kinking of the line, which can often occur with this type of lure. One must first ensure that the mount is fitted with a cylinder swivel having a diameter less than that of the body of the Devon, so that when a fish attacks, the Devon can easily shoot up the line. Since there is no rigid point to take hold of, there is considerably less likelihood of the salmon slipping the hook. The anti-kinking effect of this swivel is complete if, between the line and the end-tackle, at around 3 feet from the lure, a second good quality swivel is inserted.

There are also Devons which rotate either to the right or to the left. By using these it is also possible to limit the effects of kinking. Finally it must not be forgotten that some types of nylon are much more sensitive to this than others.

A Devon is usually attacked violently, without any shadow of doubt, and in most cases the salmon will be found with the Devon deep in its throat.

PREVIOUS PAGES *A Pacific salmon returning to its native river. It does not feed, though this will not stop it biting a lure.*

For all these reasons, and for many others, each salmon caught is a story in itself, just as with each fish that "got away." One may forget one's first cigarette, one's first dictation, or one's first tie; but just as one will not forget one's first kiss, one cannot forget one's first salmon. Indeed it is often this that converts the occasional angler to the obsessive angler. It all boils down to the truth of the saying: "the angler who thought himself the hunter is himself caught."

And sometimes this can happen on one's first fishing trip, with the first cast of the line: the famous "beginner's luck." Because, in contrast with many other species of fish that are far more fussy about the quality and presentation of bait, the salmon will bite anything – but only when he wants to bite.

For the whole of its time in the river the salmon does not feed; so it will not take bait for nutritional reasons. Why does it bite, then? That is one of the many mysteries of its behavior.

Comb the top and bottom ends of pools

All anglers have wondered about this. Such aggressive behavior is observed when it comes to the time for reproduction, the instinct which drives the salmon on upstream in its native river. This is no doubt true in the weeks preceding spawning, but fishing is not permitted at those times, and the problem does not really exist in that sense on rivers.

However it is an acknowledged fact that at each stage of its migration, when it arrives at and settles in a new pool, the salmon clears its chosen patch and chases off any intruders. Unfortunately for the angler, though, this ill humor does not last for very long. What is more, a salmon which is about to depart and leave its resting pool behind, can appear quite vicious and in a biting mood. That is why it is always advisable, when one does not know the exact place to find what one is looking for, to start by carefully combing the top and bottom ends of the pool.

Curiosity has also been expressed at the fact that a salmon will swallow a multicolored fly or a quivering Devon. What people sometimes forget is that, as far as the salmon is concerned, when it swallows such items, biting is just its way of touching. That is a possible explanation – but one might also consider this curiosity alongside the tendency many of these fish have to pounce on poplar catkins and twigs, as much as on insects swimming around on the surface.

In any case, when it comes down to it, is it really necessary to know exactly what makes a salmon bite? We might equally well ask what makes us fish? Is not the most important point the fact that the salmon may bite anything, provided it wants to do so.

Between the two wars, for instance, shrimps were rare and difficult to come by along the banks of European rivers, being a considerable distance from the ocean. To get hold of shrimps was seen as a real feat. And there were certain "old hands" who swore by nothing else, once the water temperature passed 50^{0}F, in order to attract salmon, placing particular value on the long, mobile antennae these small creatures have. In order to get round this shortage, some tried using ears of rye, painted bright red, the large tufts of which were a good imitation of shrimp antennae. The effect must have been perfect, to judge from the results achieved by those who lived through that period.

In most Norwegian rivers, on the other hand, anglers used to take great pains – before this form of fishing was banned – to cut off the antennae and front section before fixing the shrimp, painted mauve or violet, onto the hook. Norwegian anglers actually claim that unless this precaution were taken, most of the time the salmon would content themselves with picking at the shrimp without taking the hook.

It is a fact, in salmon fishing, that there are as many "truths" as there are rivers, or even stretches of river in the case of the longer ones.

The results are just as good when using spoons as when using the Devon

One angler will fish using a fly mounted on a No. 6/0; another, on the other side of the fjord, just two miles away, will be using a modest No. 2. To this we must add the predictable, not to say, superstitious, attitude of the angler who assures you that "Only the spinner works here. And it must be the right one: a white No. 3 with red tips and a black striped tail." Despite the fact that results are just as good when using a spoon as when using a Devon. And this rather crazy, or should we say magical, feature of the salmon adds charm to fishing, strengthening the cohesion of the small group that puts all its confidence in a favorite type of spoon, its lucky mascot. The spinner is no longer just a lure, it becomes the symbol of belonging to a special community. One need only poke one's nose into the box or tackle bag of a salmon angler, and on the basis of the lures it contains it is possible to reconstruct the path he has covered in his fishing career, identifying his river of origin and the grounds he moves between throughout the season.

In fact the real question is not so much "What?", as "Where?", "When?", and above all "How?" Spoon, spinner, Devon, plug, shrimp, fly, worm or deadbait ... it matters little. What is more important is to find out the river in which he fishes. The salmon will not bite anywhere. It has its behavior patterns, its hiding places,

and its habits, which continue to be a mystery, and which are passed on from generation to generation provided that the river does not change, since it can be disturbed by floods and by human activity. Thus in a 200-yard pool only 30 or 40 yards are likely to prove profitable, and these should be concentrated on persistently. It must also be noted that all these hot spots vary with the level of the water. Moreover, certain pools

The salmon fights valiantly. Here is a Chinook or "King" salmon, the largest species of Pacific salmon. The Americans fish it using the "clown", a winged lure.

only hold fish when the water level is high, while others only when the level is low. If the level is not right, it is pointless persisting.

It will be readily appreciated, therefore, that for this type of fishing, one needs to be accompanied by a friend or by a professional guide, a gillie, if one is hoping for any chance of success on a stretch of water with which one is unfamiliar or which one is visiting for the first time. Only those familiar with a particular spot will know exactly where the salmon are likely to bite.

Because of this, certain facts which on the surface

seem miraculous, if not magic – and there are many stories attached to various salmon rivers – do in fact have a rational explanation. In the mid-1960s, for instance, on one of those rare stable pools on the lower stretches of the Allier, two anglers were vying – one using a Devon, and the other a spoon – for a salmon which every now and then let them know it was still there, a sign that it was in a biting mood. This situation continued for two hours, without respite. Further along, a third angler noticed what was going on and, seeing that his fellow anglers were about to take a well-earned break to have a

snack, decided to move closer to ask them, very politely of course, whether they minded if he tried out his Devon. He did not have to cast it three times. On the second attempt, the salmon took the hook right into its mouth. It was a fine specimen weighing 17lb, just over 3ft in length. As it was later explained, the third fisherman had noticed that the other two were fishing too far out, around 22–25 ft from the bank. With a water temperature of around 41°F – it was right at the start of the season – the salmon was not going to move that far out to take the lure; it just needed to have the Devon or spoon held in front of its nose. Moreover, unknown to the first two anglers, the fish was not showing itself in exactly the same position as the one it occupied on the bottom of the pool, but a little further out and further downstream, due to the water levels. All of this was known to the knowledgeable third man, and he only needed the chance to cast his own line.

As far as the first two anglers were concerned, this was pure luck or some miracle; from the point of view of our wiser and happier friend, however, who did not try to undeceive them, it was simply the outcome of a logical approach, based on years of experience and skill.

Indeed it is a fact that all too often credit has been given to luck in salmon fishing, overlooking the essential reasons in favor of many other factors. This explains why in European rivers, where catches are few and far between, each catch is regarded as a feat, and with time that feat becomes a legend.

Another essential element is to know, or to have an instinctive awareness of, the "right moment", once the "right spot" has been identified.

The start of the season is generally the most favorable time: it is then that the largest specimens are running in all the salmon waters of Europe and elsewhere. Moreover, those fish which have not yet been disturbed are far more likely to bite than when fishing has been going on for two or three months. The end of the season, August in Norway, September in Ireland,

On salmon rivers it is necessary to identify the pathways followed by fish. A good knowledge of such places is essential for success.

THE BASIC EQUIPMENT FOR FLY FISHING

It is not everyday that you buy a rod and reel for fly fishing. Such purchases are the result of careful thought, and form part of a planned fishing program: you would not use the same equipment on the Gave as on a small river in Ireland, and you would not use the same equipment for 5–6lb grilse as for 16–24lb fish. But the choice of a fly fishing rod may also be a matter of tradition and culture: a large 16ft, two-hand rod would be just as unusual on the big rivers in Quebec as a 9ft, single-hand rod would be on the upper Allier. Yet there are valid reasons for both size of rod.

To simplify matters we can say: on wide rivers, and for long casts, use a 14–18ft two-handed rod; and use a 9–11ft single-handed rod elsewhere. But maybe we are forgetting too quickly that fly fishing, even for salmon, is simply a matter of casting. It is in the water, not in the air, that our lure will do its work. That is why there are many anglers who prefer the large rod, even when fishing in small rivers. They take the view that this gives them better control of the drifting lure, in addition to a better presentation of the fly in the right part of the water. Indeed on certain overgrown banks of a wide river a 16ft rod makes it possible to cover all sections of the water, making light work of the vegetation which can, and so often does, cause trouble near the edges.

Conversely, on wide rivers not affected by such vegetation or other obstacles near the banks, those skilled in double hauling manage perfectly well using a 10ft rod, and are able to reach distances which would do credit to those who favor long rods. Moreover, and this is a major criterion for game anglers, the struggle will be more exciting when the rod is shorter, because you will experience a closer contact with the fish. It has been stated, and repeated, that a fly reel is a secondary accessory, a simple "reservoir for the line." That is true, but it is important that this reservoir be able to hold a No. 11 line and its backing, at least 100 yards of 30lb Dacron. Finally there is some debate about whether to opt for a simple mechanism, or whether to go for a reel with a handle that can be disengaged, fitted with a very gradual brake, the latter solution being more demanding than the first.

and October in Scotland, can also be an excellent time. In France, there has been a ban on fishing at that time for some years now. One is tempted to say that this is just as well, even if some small rivers in Brittany could cope with a fishing season in the fall.

It is also better to fish when the sun is producing long shadows, at dawn or dusk, even if on occasions one hears of the famous "midday catch" of the trout angler, particularly at the start of the season. Similarly, preference should always be shown for overcast, grey skies, or alternating sun and cloud, rather than for periods of unbroken sunshine.

But these are only points of reference, or vague indicators if they are not taken in conjunction with water movements, since such factors are always of considerable importance. If a sudden downpour causes the water level to rise, this may herald a period of lean pickings for that section of the river. If the level becomes stable after a spell of flooding, this may usher in the

peak fishing period of the season. On the other hand, a long period of low water levels, even in a river that is well stocked with fish, is a guarantee that anglers will go home empty-handed and frustrated. That is why it is always a risky business planning a salmon trip too far in advance: one can do nothing to alter the weather conditions on which salmon fishing is so dependent.

Thus the ideal day would seem to be a rainy morning at the start of the season, with alternating showers and tentative bright spells, just enough for the water level to be kept topped up. From time to time the newly arrived fish will show themselves, breaking the surface of the water with a timid dorsal fin. A sunny afternoon in August, on the other hand, on a river whose level is falling, would have nothing to offer. And yet.

It was in August 1980 on a trip to newly discovered Norway, a land full of promise for the angler, and offering breathtaking scenery. Unfortunately the water levels had continued to fall for three weeks. The furious torrent

FLY FISHING FOR SALMON IN OPEN WATER

This is the most common practice on our large fast-running rivers, and contrasts with what one might call the "greased line" and the surface fly method used by anglers in parts of Europe. But these two techniques are of course dependent on the submerged fly, since the dry method is only really used on certain rivers in Quebec as well as in Scotland and Ireland.

It makes it possible to fish the middle and deep layers of water, and requires specially adapted equipment: a fully submerged line, or a line with a sinking point. A good compromise is provided by intermediate lines which float when greased, or at least stay near the surface, and which become submerged, when not greased, without actually sinking to the bottom. This means they can be used equally as a "greased line" and for open water fly fishing. In the latter case one adapts moderately or fully sinking end-tackle, of the sort that is now commercially available in a number of forms. This compromise solution enables the beginner to familiarize himself with salmon fishing, using the fly, without having to incur too great an expenditure at the start.

This technique is practiced primarily on the fast-flowing sections of rivers. Here one uses flies with fairly stiff fibers: top quality hackle flanges, and wings made from badger, calf, marten or fox fur. The conventional models, which each angler can adapt and make to suit

himself, such as the Jock Scott, the Black Doctor or the Lemon Gray, have stood the test in waters around the world. Indeed, for this type of fishing there is no such thing as the "right fly." What *is* important is that the angler have confidence in his lure. If one wishes to fish more extensively, and in deeper water, it is possible to use tube-flies made with a brass body, and fitted with a treble hook.

The line is cast three-quarters downstream, fairly tight, so that the fly will fish as soon as it hits the water; it is then allowed to drift, maintaining contact, as it is carried by the current. Its descent may be accompanied by a steady movement of the tip of the rod in order to accentuate its movement, reinforcing the impression of its being a live fly. If a fish has been spotted, an effort must be made to fish at the tightest angle possible, even if this means a considerable length of line. This actually enables the fly to move very slowly, or to stop in the area where salmon are to be found.

When a fish bites, there is not a visual indication. It may however manifest itself in the form of a sharp tug, or an unexpected slackening of the line. A sustained retrieval, which must never be too early, will guarantee a catch. This is when the best part of the fishing experience begins: struggling with a salmon caught on a fly rod and trying every trick it can to escape.

In order to spawn, the salmon swims upstream a considerable distance.

SALMON FISHING USING A SURFACE FLY

This form of fishing, as we have mentioned, has nothing to do with dry fly fishing; it is also known as "greased line" fishing, the preferred technique of French anglers who fish the calmer stretches of rivers upstream of dams: the "ponds". But it can also be used anywhere else salmon are likely to be found outside the main flow of water. It is done 8–15 inches beneath the water surface, using a floating line or a greased intermediate line. In other words, it is mostly a visible fishing method, which also adds to its charm.

Since there is no current, it is up to the angler to make the fly move around, but he must also choose a model which is able to vibrate at the slightest stimulus.

This explains why these flies are made in very soft fibers: feathers from the side of a peacock, golden pheasant tufts, soft squirrel fur. Moreover the rough appearance of their bodies, usually in the form of silver tinsel encased boar's hair, adds further to the impression of life that these flies display as soon as they touch the water. Mounted on a single hook, the large models used in fast-flowing water are only suited to a No. 2 or even a No. 1 hook, while the smaller models can go down to a No. 8 or even a No. 10 hook.

On the calmer parts of rivers where this technique is used, the line is cast slightly upstream or at right-angles to the bank, without forgetting first of all to examine the immediate vicinity at the edge of the bank where one is standing; one then establishes contact with the fly, lightly pulling on the line. In contrast with fishing in fast flowing currents, this is not a trust-to-luck method, but an active method which requires concentration and accuracy in handling the fly. In order to use it to best advantage, and to cause all its components to vibrate, it is necessary for the left hand to impose alternating pulling and release movements as it retrieves the line, in conjunction with movements of the tip of the rod.

In most instances you will see the salmon rising, or failing that you will see the boiling of the water produced as it attacks the fly. Just before striking, it is a good idea to wait a short time until the fish has taken up its normal position again. Experience shows that more fish are lost through hasty striking than through delayed striking. The first rush of the salmon taken by surprise in this way can be very violent; it is better not to check this reaction, especially if the flies used are unsuited to end-tackle in excess of 18 or 30/100e. Rather you should be "courteous to the fish," as anglers from Quebec often say, allowing it to take as much line as it wants until it stops of its own volition.

encountered on arrival was reduced to a stream running over a bed of rocks. Norwegian friends had already given up fishing under those circumstances, except for mackerel, in the waters that poured into the nearby fjord. They had to restrain themselves from laughing at those who set off for the river, in which there only remained two or three slightly deeper holes that one might attempt to fish in.

That afternoon was spent in the fjord. Leiff was the guide in those first attempts as an angler. Anything he said was taken as gospel. On that occasion, however, he was ignored, despite his mocking, and was left alone fishing for mackerel, as his protégé made his way toward the river, toward the "Little Ditch," one pool that could still be fished. Wearing Polaroid sunglasses – Leiff had recommended this device for spotting fish on those very first fishing trips – and with rod in hand, a stop was made, urged by some unidentified instinct, only a few yards before the envisaged spot.

And there "he" was, where he had no right to be, just about three feet beneath the surface, between two pools. An August afternoon, in full sunlight. The repeated movement of his caudal fin indicated that he might be in a biting mood. As the spinner passed by him for the first time, it seemed as if he moved a little. Perhaps it was just an illusion? On the second attempt, without hurrying, just like a trout with a minute pupa, he swallowed the spoon. The ensuing struggle lasted no more than 10-15 minutes. The high temperature and the absence of any depth of water no doubt explained the brevity of this encounter. What is more, this particular 26lb fish remains the biggest salmon the writer has ever caught. It is also a fact that today he would have no chance of gaining such a trophy, for the simple reason that he no longer fishes under those conditions. Sometimes one needs to be naive and inexperienced in order to succeed with this most individual fish.

Accept failure as the norm, and success as a rare reward

Even if salmon fishing requires a good knowledge of the habits of this species and of the waters in which it is to be found, and even if the use of a certain type of lure is in part responsible for achieving good results, the attitude of the angler is equally a decisive factor for success. Salmon fishing means accepting failure as the norm, and success as a reward, always the exception, for

obeying a whole series of requirements: technique, tactics, and approach. Patience, determination, and obstinacy are the best weapons in the salmon fisher's armory as he moves up and down the river bank.

If it is recognized that a salmon will only bite at certain moments in the day, once it has settled in its pool, the angler has the choice between two tactics, depending on his preferences, his temperament, or the requirements of the stretch of water being fished.

Fishing stone by stone, with tackle gauged to a fraction of an inch

The first approach is to take up a position at a pool and to stay there for the whole of the fishing session. This is the solution adopted by some sedentary, home-loving anglers in our public waters, who are able to cast the same lure all day long from the same spot, throughout the season. This is an extreme case, but real enough, and harks back to the days when people were far less mobile than they are today. These anglers, usually older than average, have a thorough knowledge of their favorite pool, and if you can get on the right side of them, little by little they will reveal to you how that particular spot is to be read and fished.

But this may also be the fishing method of the travelling angler who has rented a stretch of water, sometimes well in advance, which turns out to have a single pool in which fishing is really practicable. If it is well stocked, and the fish are in a biting mood, he will have a wonderful time there, because at the end of two or three days he will know the spot stone by stone and will gauge his tackle to a fraction of an inch. If, on the other hand, salmon are not present, or are in hiding because the water is shallow as the result of the lack of rain, then it can be catastrophic, and anyone not prepared for such an eventuality will suffer the frustration that can go with this method of static fishing. But one can also go home empty-handed from the Tay in Scotland, from the Orkla in Norway and from the Allier or Gave in France, as the writer knows only too well from his personal experience. It is just that this is a rare occurrence.

The big advantage of our public waters – the salmon license gives access, in France, to several hundred miles of river banks – even if they only contain small numbers

The salmon moves little. You have to pass the lure right in front of its nose.

SALMON FISHING USING WORM BAIT

Unfairly described by many of those who have never used it, provided it is carried out in a game fishing context, and not from a static position, salmon fishing using worm bait is a method that demonstrates considerable skill, and is often profitable. This no doubt explains its more or less universal nature: you will come across it on all salmon rivers except, in France, on the Allier. Both for shallow water fishing and for deep water fishing it can become a compulsive activity.

A relatively long flexible 11–12ft casting rod is used, and this can also be used for fishing using shrimp bait which, like the worm, is a little fragile. Use single No. 2/0 hooks, with barbs on the shank to grip the worms. A first worm is threaded onto the hook, then a second at right-angles; because of the uncoordinated movements this produces, it has the attractive effect of a small octopus. The weighting is usually attached to a paternoster link, employing a swivel with a stop of a diameter that is somewhat less than that of the line, on which you pinch two or three pieces of shot, depending on the weight required.

The difficulty of this technique resides in the fact that it is both a casting method and a ledgering method, at one and the same time, requiring a number of qualities which can at times be contradictory: flexibility and power for casting at a great distance without damaging the bait, accuracy, and sensitivity. It involves fishing the worm right in front of the fish, often at a considerable distance from the angler himself. In this context it is not always easy to identify a fish taking the bait, and to distinguish it from the hook merely touching the bottom. Because while the salmon sometimes takes the bait with an unmistakable snatch, it may also do so discreetly, content to nibble at the worm and to clamp it in its mouth without actually swallowing it. If in doubt, you should strike, and this must be more resolute and pronounced the greater the distance involved.

of salmon, is that they make it possible for the second category of angler, the "river runners," to give free reign to their love of movement. Such anglers do not stay in the same place: hardly have they reached one pool, than they have already decided which pool to move on to. They maintain, often rightly, that if a salmon is in a biting mood, it will attack a lure when it is presented for the first time, and that in light of this it is pointless to persist too long at the same pool. Rarely do they cast more than three times at the same spot, unless they are sure, from the evidence of their own eyes, that a fish is within their reach. Even then they will not hang about all day "treading water." They are temperamentally unsuited to keeping still. However, whatever the approach taken, the method opted for must never be at the expense of basic courtesy. If other anglers arrive on the spot, the "sedentary" angler will stop for a short while, or move down the pool a little faster than usual to allow his fellows to set up. Conversely, the "river runner" will wait until an angler already in action has finished moving down the pool, or invites the newcomer to try his luck. Under no circumstances will he take up a

What is is that makes a salmon take a shrimp? It is not hunger. It may be the movement or even the smell which attracts it.

position downstream of an angler who is already in place. These basic rules, passed down from one generation to the next on all salmon rivers, are also part of the make-up of the rounded angler.

Whether he is a sedentary angler or a "river runner," an obsessive or only an occasional angler, the fascination that causes him to cast time and time again, without asking questions, is the same, convinced that he is justified in the choices he has made. And it is the same obstinacy that allows him to believe, with each cast, that this is the one that will produce the hoped for attack, even if for many seasons, he has not caught a single fish in the pool he is fishing. He believes this, despite the statistics that tell us that in French waters only one quarter of a salmon is caught per angler per year, and that only one in three foreign fishing trips abroad can be expected to provide good conditions.

He fishes more with his heart than with his head – and relies as much on his gut feelings as on his hands. He reminds himself that everything is possible – the big fish, and what may often involve a fierce struggle, – which helps him to while away the many hours of patient waiting.

For all these reasons, salmon fishing is more a way of life than catching fish.

SALMON FISHING USING SHRIMP BAIT

Salmon do not feed in rivers, but this does not prevent them from attacking worms or shrimp bait offered by the angler.

You can use the small gray shrimp, attached live to a single hook; this is how a number of Irish and Spanish anglers approach the subject. But the most common method is to use a 3-5 inch cluster of shrimps that have been boiled and preserved in glycerine. The most often-used form of attachment, for presentation of the bait, is to thread the shrimp on a small metal shaft with a loop that can be fitted to the line. You can use a treble, No. 1 or 2, or two No. 8 hooks, remembering that the shrimp hunts with its head forward, i.e. the wrong way round. In order to ensure that the bait is secure, you can wind some fine copper around it. As with worm bait, weighting is on a paternoster link, some 3ft from the shrimp.

A fairly long rod will enable you to cast the bait without damaging it, and to cause it to move around, followed by brief stops, imitating its backward swimming

motion. When a salmon takes this bait it may be with considerable force, and without any shadow of doubt as it swallows the shrimp. Sometimes, however, as with worm bait, it may hesitate and nibble at the shrimp, without properly biting and following the bait as it moves about. It is also possible that the salmon's presence goes completely unnoticed, until you retrieve the almost completely shredded shrimp.

This is a technique used in the middle and toward the end of the season, in water that is by now fairly warm. In some areas its use is strictly regulated: in Norway, the use of shrimp bait has been completely banned since 1988.

Moreover it has often been observed that if a salmon does not bite more or less at once, when shrimp bait is used to attract it, it can become nervous and will not bite again for many hours. Some anglers even think that using shrimp bait can have the effect of breaking up a pool, which may explain the bans that have been imposed on this technique.

TROUT

GILBERT BORDES

Salmo trutta fario! With so splendid a name, how could the trout be anything but a highborn lady, shining star of creation's finest rivers, dream fish worshiped by millions of anglers. The trout is in a class of its own. Watch one swim, gracefully, effortlessly, with sinuous movements of its whole body. This is no carp or roach, which gives two or three flicks of its tail, then coasts through the water. The trout is a natural dancer, advancing with smooth, elegant precision. When it lies in wait for its prey in mid-stream, it lies almost motionless, keeping station with consummate ease. This is a sight not to be missed. Approach the river bank with infinite care. There she is, just beneath the surface, watching out for passing insects. You can make out her greenish-brown back and the black and red spots on her flank; her slightly elliptical eyes have a presence not found in lesser fish, they express her lively personality.

One can observe trout hour upon hour. It was a passion as a child. The stream that flowed close to the house cast a spell; school had to take second place. An apprenticeship was served catching minnows and gudgeon. Of course, the magnificent fish one had learned to stalk were still out of reach. Sometimes, a taciturn angler would come up the river, casting an artificial fly made by winding a cockerel feather round the shank of a hook. On occasion, he would lift the lid of his creel and allow smaller anglers to admire those tantalizing fish, resplendent on their bed of damp bracken.

Then, one day, it was the youngster's turn to experience the indescribable thrill of playing a trout, a moment he has never forgotten: seven at the time, and there had just been a storm. Minnows had been abandoned as the water was colored and instead he pretended to fish for trout, letting the worm be carried along by the current. Suddenly, the rod was almost snatched from his grasp. The line held and he saw, in an eddy on the surface, the fish struggling to break free. As luck would have it, he managed to draw the fish over the shingle on the bank. There the fish managed to throw the hook and began struggling toward the water, while the angler, equally desperate, shuffled it back to dry land with hands and feet. He returned home like a conquering hero. The fish weighed almost half a pound.

From that day on, gudgeon and crayfish lost their charm! Trout became an obsession: drawn in exercise books, shaped in modeling clay. He taught himself to tie

artificial flies with feathers from a rooster, but his real speciality was fishing with natural baits, worms and insects. Fly fishing would have to wait.

Since then trout have been caught by the thousand, each time with the same delight, the same enthusiasm. Their ephemeral beauty, fading the moment they die, is an enduring source of wonder. A trout fresh drawn from the water is a masterpiece of color, the sight of its iridescent flanks flashing in the sunlight is a handsome reward for the angler.

As a schoolboy, he would regularly visit the family doctor for a week's sick note. He invented pains of all kinds, and could tell from the malicious twinkle in the old man's eye that he did not believe a word of it: he would nevertheless reach for his headed notepaper and write that such a state of health called for a week's rest. Rest indeed! The young angler would be up at daybreak and would fish through until nightfall. His idea of utter and complete paradise!

Large numbers of trout were caught, partly because the river held an abundance of fish, partly because there were few other fishermen about. During the adolescent years, he was never short of pocket money.

Since then he has fished in almost every country in the world, catching trout in every conceivable circumstance: the magnificent rivers of Canada and Finland, for example, but he has found nothing that draws him like the streams and rivers of his native Corrèze. They are bound up with a happy youth and he returns to them year after year. They hold no secrets for him now and he

Trout rising slowly to take a floating insect. In "sipping" the fly, it makes only a small disturbance: a good sign.

A rainbow trout clearing the water, possibly hunting fully adult insects such as sedges.

The trout has taken a fly and, turning, makes for the bottom. Now is the moment to strike, but be careful: better strike a little late than a little early.

Trout about to take a fly. The fisherman must resist striking until the fish has taken the fly and turned.

can read the mood of the fish and what tomorrow's weather will bring. Water is a mirror foretelling changes in the order of nature.

There are many rivers one is happy to fish, but only two with which one entertains real love affairs, so different one from the other, yet perfectly complementary. The Vézère is the more faithful of the two, and the more turbulent. From Treignac, where it flows among huge boulders, to the calmer reaches at Uzerche, not a yard of bank, not a swim is unfamiliar. The Vézère is a deceptive river, always putting on a smiling face, but often disappointing. It often seems to reserve its finest trout for other fishermen, yet we are inseparable. When all is said and done, the Vézère is preferred to the Corrèze. The latter is a real trout river, with currents running close to the bank over a bed of golden gravel. But how capricious she can be! How often has the challenge been met? The Corrèze is a demanding river to fish, fickle in its moods. Some days, the trout seem ready to take anything with gay abandon. At other times, for no apparent reason, the swims are empty and you have to exercise all your skills if you are to avoid going home with an empty creel.

The trout has been the biggest single influence on the author's life. But for this fish, he would not be what he is today; his life-style would be totally different. And he has developed an intimate knowledge and insight into the ways of the trout.

You will doubtless be aware that the trout is a member of the salmon family, a close cousin of the Atlantic

Trout hunting nymphs. It lurks at mid-depth, so as not to let any escape.

Typical behavior of a trout feeding on hatching nymphs, the final stage of aquatic life before the larva or free-swimming pupa transforms to an adult insect. Quite different from the way a trout breaks the surface to take a dry fly!

A fish has broken the surface with its dorsal fin. Try fishing with an emerging nymph pattern. It is unlikely to take a dry fly.

The fish returns to the bottom to devour its prey. Wait a few moments before trying to tempt it again.

salmon (*Salmo salar*), with which it is able to cross-breed albeit rarely: the sea trout, which is the same species as the brown trout, interbreeds more commonly with the salmon. The trout is found everywhere in France, except in certain lowland rivers, where the water is too warm. There is a large number of different "varieties". Each river has its indigenous strain, which is why the introduction of eggs or fry from Scotland or Norway is not in the interests of our own fish, so perfectly adapted to their environment. This accounts for the disappearance of the big trout of the Dordogne. When they reached a certain size, fish of this strain would travel downstream to warmer waters, where, thriving on smaller fish, they grew to record sizes. When the dams were built, they could no longer find suitable spawning grounds and have since all but disappeared. On the other hand, trout hatched from eggs whose forebears roamed the fjords of Norway are often migratory by nature and do not adapt to the tougher conditions of running water, where food is relatively scarce. Our native fish are, of course, perfectly at home in these circumstances.

There is also a lake-dwelling form of brown trout. The fisheries department is perhaps remiss in not making more of this superb fish, which could be introduced to many artificial lakes. Trout of this kind feed on young fish (perch fry mainly, as the artificial fluctuations in the water level of reservoirs inhibits the population growth of bait fish) and are sometimes able to spawn in small tributary streams.

THE RIGHT ROD FOR NATURAL BAIT FISHING

Free-lining or touch-ledgering, the latter using various small weights as appropriate, are two excellent techniques for natural bait fishing. In streams, the fish are small and can be caught at a rod's length, using a fairly long rod for maximum control. Precision is vital, particularly at the start of the season, when the trout are still in hiding. A carbon fiber rod, 15–17 ft in length, is quite adequate. Telescopic rods are now available, which can be adjusted for length and have a very satisfactory action. When fishing streams with a lot of overhanging branches, rods with the line threaded through internally are preferable.

On wider rivers, the swims are much bigger and you need to cast long distances to reach the fish. A short rod – between 12 and 13 ft – is more suitable, again with a very light line. A small, light-weight reel is best. A fixed-spool reel will do, even if experts tend to recommend other types.

16/100ths is quite adequate for the line. Anything thicker would rub against the inner walls of the rod and hinder casting. The leader should be of 12 or 14/100ths, the size of the hook depending on the bait you intend to use (8 for a worm or grasshopper, 12 to 16 for a wax moth larva or natural fly). How you weight the line depends on the strength of the current: you will probably need between two and five 8 shot. As the depth of water is bound to vary from place to place, you will have to fish without a float, but you can use a small fluorescent indicator to help you locate your line at a glance.

Sensitivity is the essence of this style of fishing. The art is to cast your line into the swim and guide it in such a way that the bait is carried by the current. By holding the line in your hand, you should be able to feel the slightest bite and know just when to strike.

The sea trout is another variety which, like the salmon, makes it way to the sea after spending the early years of its life in fresh water. It returns to the rivers to spawn in the fall. Taking this into account, French law permits fishing for sea trout until the end of November in recognized "sea trout rivers." The spawning of this species is hindered by the building of power-station dams, and the pollution of estuaries which forms a toxic barrier the fish are reluctant to cross.

The familiar rainbow trout, large numbers of which are introduced to our rivers each year in readiness for the new season, will not be discussed in depth. Scientists no longer consider it a trout, but class it as a member of the Genus Oncorhynchus, which includes all the Pacific species of salmon. This is quite logical when you consider that the rainbow originates from the American Northwest and that many varieties are anadromous (i.e. they live in salt water and enter rivers to spawn). It cross-breeds occasionally with Pacific salmon, spawning, like them, in late winter and spring, whereas a cross between a rainbow and a brown trout is very rare, clearly demonstrating the genetic distance between the two fish.

The rainbow trout is nevertheless a permanent feature of our fishing environment and a superb fighting fish when it has grown up in the wild. It is less fussythan the brown trout and will tolerate higher temperatures. Strains which have not been weakened by generations of the fish-farm regime are excellent for stocking lakes, where they rapidly put on weight.

THREE NATURAL BAITS

In the early part of the season, worms make excellent bait, but you have to choose the right sort. The common-or-garden earthworm (*Lumbricus*), easily recognized by its flat, lighter-colored tail, breaks easily. Dung worms, which release a yellowish fluid, are not much good either. The most suitable kind are found in rotting organic matter. To ensure a good supply, all you need do is bury some sheets of newspaper in the garden and water them regularly.

Really big worms are only suitable for touch-ledgering or more static ledgering. For investigating swims, 2 or 3 inch specimens are quite big enough. They will keep well in a can with a few small air holes. Let them scour in some damp moss a few days before you use them and they will be less fragile.

A second early-season bait is the wax moth larva, a white grub similar to the larva of the caddis fly, the adult of which is a parasite of bee-hives. Wax moth larvae can be kept for several days, but it is essential that they be fresh and succulent.

Another excellent bait, specially in April and May, is a minnow, which should be 2 to 3 inches in length. Minnows can be attached to special deadbait tackle and used for bait casting. For this type of fishing, a single hook is preferable. The technique is slightly different in this case. The minnow should still be alive and the art is to give it additional animation by regular tugs on the line. A minnow may provoke a big trout which is indifferent to all other baits.

Various trout baits: grasshoppers, wax moth larvae, worms and, for bigger customers, small bait fish.

FOLLOWING PAGES *A brook trout, a fish which behaves not unlike a brown trout.*

Returning to our wild native species, the brown trout, its future does not appear very bright. Several successive years of drought have lowered the water level in our rivers, making the fall migration to the spawning grounds difficult. Dams for hydro-electric power generation are having the same effect. It is just not true to say that trout can reproduce satisfactorily in large rivers. Even if they manage to find suitable gravel beds, the alevin are bound to be snapped up by predators the moment they emerge.

It is vital that the fish have access to the headwaters, where the spring-fed streams are of constant temperature, if we are to encourage the native strains of trout we really want in our rivers. The need to build fish passes is therefore obvious. The trout is a demanding fish and will not tolerate pollution. Agricultural fertilizers, insecticides and fungicides tend to run off into rivers and have destroyed many of the aquatic insects on which the fish feed. Mistakes have been made. Ill-considered stocking of reared fish has been more to the detriment of native fish than for their good. Besides the genetic corruption of native strains, the introduction of foreign species has been undertaken without considering the capacity of the new environment to receive them. Given the already limited food supply, the excessive numbers of fish introduced tend to be under-nourished and small in size. The entire food chain should have been taken into account, and appropriate measures taken to foster it. Trout may be poor breeders when compared with members of the carp family, but the survival rate of their off-

The shoot: the fly line shoots out over the water, allowing the leader to turn over and delicately land the fly in the current.

Try to prevent drag: the line may be carried away faster than the fly, pulling the lure downstream.

The roll cast: the rod is raised to "11 o'clock," the line beginning to billow out behind.

The rod is moved sharply forward and down, causing the line to roll out over the water.

spring will be much higher if the right conditions can be recreated.

Artificial introduction into the wild of large numbers of young fish upsets the age pyramid. The big fish die and are not replaced. As soon as they reach the size prescribed by law, the trout caught are kept by the ever-increasing number of anglers. Thus, the few adult fish which survive are insufficient to guarantee natural reproduction, and further batches of artificially bred fish have to be released.

One answer would be to increase the legal size for caught fish. Nowadays, trout fishing is not an expensive hobby and though the law sets a limit on the number of fish that may be taken in a day, it imposes no restriction on the number of anglers allowed to fish the river.

Unless such a limit is imposed, the other measures will prove worthless.

Undoubtedly, such restrictions and constraints are a pity, as freedom is the very essence of fishing, but the survival of the wild trout is at stake. Our rivers are fragile systems, symbolic of nature's abundance. Some sacrifices on our part should not be too much to ask. Perhaps we should now start to consider more the effects of man as a predator disturbing the balance and depleting the genetic resources of the quarry we hold in such respect. Increasingly fishermen in such countries as America, Britain, and New Zealand are recognizing

FOLLOWING PAGES *A magnificent sea trout, migratory form of the brown trout. It gives great sport when taken on a fly.*

The left hand has an important part to play, imparting fine adjustments to the line, tensioning the rod, and hauling the line.

Fishing across and down a fast stream: the cast.

Fishing across and down a fast stream: raising the rod to prevent a bow developing between angler and fly.

A bite. The fish is hooked and the rod bends. The reward for several hours of patient fishing.

Casting. To make things easier for the beginner, we start with 5 yards of line laid out on the water, extended by the current. The fisherman stands facing his line, the rod held horizontally.

The back cast. The rod is lifted smartly, bringing the line with it. Pulling in line with the left hand accelerates the take-off. (This is the first part of the double haul technique). The rod is stopped at "one o'clock."

His rod now in an upright position, the fisherman must not be in a hurry. The airborne line flies out behind and begins to straighten. Eventually it begins to pull on the rod tip.

Now is the moment for the forward cast. The taut line pulls on the rod, which stores energy then releases it as the line shoots out ahead. The rod is checked at "10 o'clock."

The line shoots forward, while the rod remains stationary. The line held in the left hand is released and shoots out through the rings, adding distance to the cast.

The line is at full stretch. The fisherman dips the tip of the rod to reduce disturbance. The fly lands delicately on the water, imitating the behavior of a real insect.

their enjoyment of the challenge the trout presents is not lessened by safely returning undamaged fish to the water. "Catch and release" as this growing practice is termed is a fitting salute to a worthy adversary who can then provide us with sport on another day, a little wiser perhaps but maintaining our essential gene pool.

It is in terms of trout fishing that each year we experience the changing seasons. With the coming of spring, witness the first green shoots on a sheltered stretch of river bank; enjoy the explosion of greenery in April and May, then endure the long hot days of summer, which drive the denizens of the river into hiding. The first rains in the fall bring about a regeneration. The trout make their way upstream, leaping rapids as they obey the call of the spring waters, an instinct which impels them ever further in search of clean gravel beds in which to spawn. Each season requires a different fishing technique, and a great deal of pleasure is denied those who fish at only one time of year.

The year begins with the opening of the trout-fishing season, on the first Saturday in March. The days are lengthening and winter is on the way out, though there may still be some sharp frosts. The trout are fairly

Fishing a fast-flowing river is an exhilarating experience. Short casts are essential, as the main problem is drag on the fly.

relaxed, slowly recovering their strength after their great fall migration and spawning. Food is still in short supply and though the fish tend to remain in seclusion, they are keeping their weather eye open. Should a worm come drifting along on the current, they will not hesitate to take it. This is the time for natural bait fishing, a relatively simple technique in small streams, but more complicated in larger rivers, where observing the waiting trout is more difficult.

The hierarchy of a river is absolute. The big fish occupy the best swims, places of safety where the current brings a plentiful supply of food. The most desirable stations are sheltered spots on the edge of the stream, rocks, and hollows under banks. The smaller fish have to make do with the poorer, more exposed stretches of water.

At the beginning of the season, they are often the more active, not having taken part in the winter spawning. To avoid hooking them, you need to fish with great accuracy, picking only the best swims. In streams, however, there are always large numbers of very young trout in evidence.

Try to avoid letting the fish swallow the worm, or you will have to kill it to recover the hook. You can avoid this problem by striking at the first bite and will not necessarily lose many fish, even if the worm is

fairly long. A fish hooked in the lip suffers no more damage than if he were taken on a fly.

On several occasions, the season's fishing begins with snow on the ground. In these intensely bright conditions, wear a white over-garment as camouflage. The first days of the season are always fruitful if you can only land your bait in the right spot. The trout have not been disturbed for several months and are in an unusually trusting mood.

Early April: a time of plenty

March is usually a wet month, and there is often a last cold snap. Wintry weather is not propitious for fishing. Warm days are better, even if it is raining. Late March brings a change. The days draw out and April often comes in with gusty winds to disturb the surface and sudden spells of hot sunshine favorable to insect life. Spring has arrived in all its abundance. Lurking under stones, the fragile caddis fly larvae are fat and succulent. The trout leave their hiding places and venture out into the stream. The larvae of aquatic insects become increasingly active as they approach the final stage of their metamorphosis. As you fish with caddis bait, be aware that the fish, too, are ranging further afield. The early-season swims and hiding-holes are less productive. Try swims on the margins of the current, the tail-end of rapids, places where the fish can keep watch over a promising territory without tiring themselves fighting the current.

As they become more aggressive trout can be fished for with lures. A spoon may be of little value in early March, but by April circumstances have changed.

The trout is a great fighter. When a fish leaps, the angler should be ready to yield line. This is when the line or hook hold is most likely to break.

BAIT CASTING TECHNIQUE

A rod as short as 3 ft 6 in is often called for when fishing small streams with no elbow room. On rivers, a longer rod, say 5 ft, will enable you to cast further. A fixed-spool reel is ideal for retrieving line rapidly: they are designed to wind in between 20 and 30 inches of line for each turn of the handle. There are some very light, yet highly reliable, reels on the market. Your line should be 16/100ths line, or 18/100ths if you are a beginner.

Take a good selection of spoons. Those with a wide spinning vane "fly" through the water and rotate well in smooth patches of water. The longer, narrower ones exert less pull and should be reserved for fishing in strong currents where the fish are hugging the bed.

Color is also an important factor. Some days, fish will prefer silvery spoons; on others, they will go for black or more exotically colored lures. Do not necessarily stick to a model that has proved successful in the past: the fish may well have gone off it.

The technique is relatively simple, the difficulty being to land your spinner on just the right spot. In calm water, you can cast upstream; in turbulent water, it is better to fish diagonally up and across the river, or fish downstream.

Fishing with undulating lures and spinners: two quite distinct techniques

A spinner needs to be cast accurately, upstream of the swim to be investigated. In retrieving the line, the aim is to keep the lure turning close to the bottom. The shape of the spinning vane is of the utmost importance, since it determines the depth at which the lure travels through the water and its rotation speed.

To attract fish, a spinner does not need to rotate quickly, but it must turn at the slightest prompting and keep turning when the fisherman relaxes the pressure on the line to let it sink toward the bottom.

Small spoons and undulating lures are readily taken by big trout, but they are not presented in the same way as spinners. The trick is to impart to them the jerky movements of an injured fish, rather as one would when using a plug. There are floating models which dive under water whenever the fisherman retrieves and resurface when he relaxes the pressure. These are suitable for fishing shallow swims and along the margins of the main stream.

Three wet flies for one fish: tail fly, dropper, and bob

Spring is also the time to try a wet fly. Trout feed mainly on aquatic larvae (nymphs) which venture out into the current prior to their final metamorphosis. The fish station themselves on the margins of fast stretches of water, keeping watch. Try attaching three wet flies to your leader, the tail fly being the heaviest. It should drift along the bottom, with the dropper at mid-depth and the bob just below the surface. The bob fly may even "bob" in the water surface, like a fly struggling in the surface film, hence its name. Position yourself at the head of a pool, an extensive swim where trout may be lying anywhere. Cast toward the opposite bank, leaving some slack in the line to allow the flies to sink, then take up the slack so that the flies drift slowly downstream. The current will cause the feather fibers to vibrate. The take will be positive, felt as a strong tug. There is no need to strike; the fish will have hooked itself. Work downstream, combing the current by lengthening your cast as necessary to search the water. If the current is fairly strong there is no point in imparting additional movement to the flies. In slow-running water, some fishermen draw on the line with a regular movement of the left hand. When the line has completed its drift downstream, it should be retrieved slowly (this is often the moment a fish takes), then cast again.

Wet fly fishing can be successful at any time of year, as long as the water temperature is high enough for aquatic larvae to be active.

When the nymphs hatch into adult insects, trout rise to the surface to feed. This is the time to fish with a dry fly, a technique which allows you to see the fish break surface to take the bait.

There are two possible methods. The first is to position yourself on the bank and wait until you see a fish rise to take a fly. When this occurs, attempt to identify the insect that was taken and look for a suitable imitation in your fly box. When casting to a fish, you should

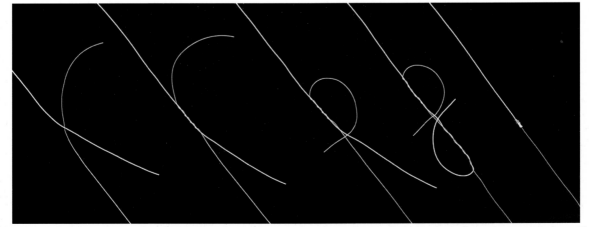

The blood knot, ideal for joining two lengths of nylon when making a leader.

RIGHT *Joining the leader to the line using a needle knot. Modern alternatives gaining popularity include the use of nylon monofilament braid which is drawn up over the end of the fly line and secured with a thin plastic tube or glue.*

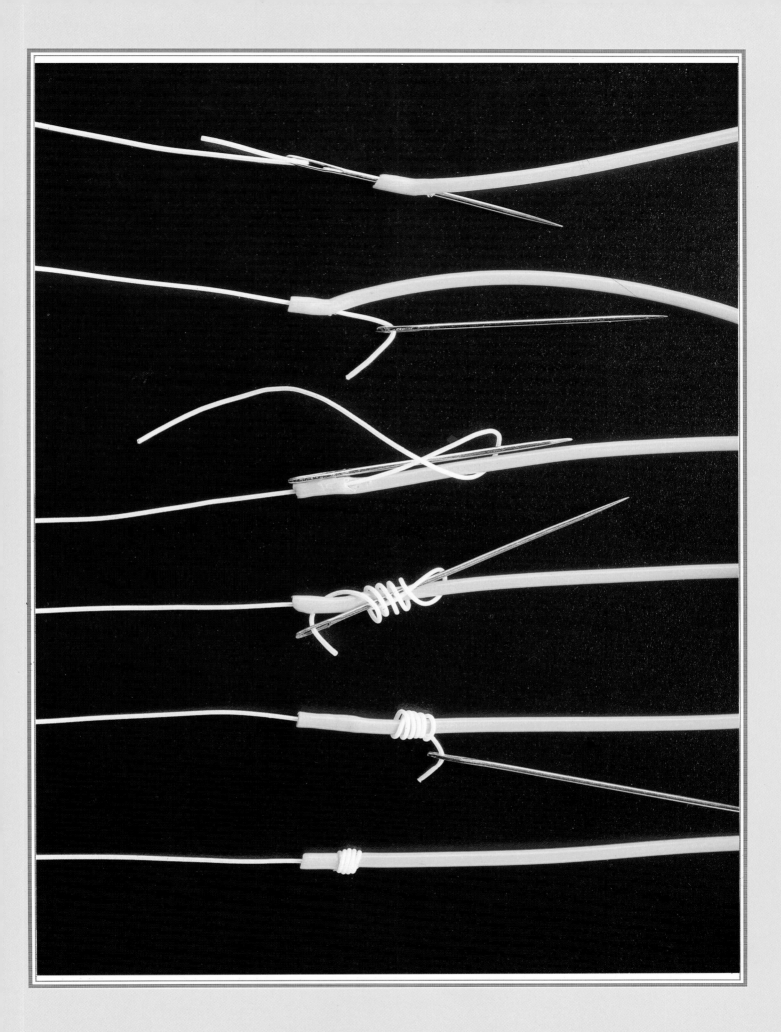

ensure your presence is not detected and try to land the fly delicately just upstream of the fish, which will be intent on the surface. If the selection was correct and the fish not alarmed, it will take the fly without hesitation.

The second method is more effective in a mountain stream or fast-flowing river, where it is possible to pin-point the position of the fish. The fly, often a general representation model, is cast to land on possible lies, without waiting for a fish to rise. This is a favorite style of fishing, since you need to be on the alert for the slightest clue to the whereabouts of your quarry. The dry fly season begins in April, but at this stage favorable moments come and go very quickly. It is possible to catch several fish in just a few minutes, but this is no time for niceties, as the fish will stop feeding as suddenly as they began. Then you will have to wait patiently, on the bank of an apparently empty river, hoping for another short burst of collective madness.

June: time to take your holidays, the trout are ready and waiting

June is the best month, the ideal time for the trout fisherman to take his holidays. The fish take up station in the stream, actively feeding on nymphs, surface insects and small fish.

In June, the artificial fly comes into its own. Get to the river early in the morning, when the sun is just beginning to warm up the surface of the water. The different species of fly hatch out in rapid succession: mayfly in slow-moving rivers, ecdyonuridae in faster-moving waters, tricoptera and a wide range of ephemeroptera, all on the water at the same time. The trout feast on them all day long. However, as the summer advances and the

Streamers are not usually patterned on any specific creature, but their profile and pulsating action through the water suggest small fish and other food, as well as provoking aggression or curiosity.

SELECTING A FLY

In fast-flowing rivers with narrow runs, trout do not have time to study floating insects and will snap at anything drifting past. A suitable choice is a general representation fly which floats well, neutral gray hackle with a red or yellow body. A fly of this sort is not patterned on any specific insect. Short casts are called for, so you need to be gentle in approaching the fish. The fly and short part of the leader must land accurately, just in front of the trout's nose.

In calmer waters and big rivers, trout are more selective. They patrol their swims, taking time to study the insects that come their way. In this case, closer representation is called for: the artificial fly must conform to the outline, color and size of the insect on which the fish are feeding. Ephemeroptera are simulated by spiders and up-winged artificials, tricoptera by sedges — flies with a tuft of hair or feather fibers tied to lie back

along the hook in imitation of wings.

In mid-summer, trout often turn their attention to ants. To get a bite in this case, it is vital to emulate the swollen appearance of the ant's abdomen.

The level at which the fly floats in the water is another key factor. Adult insects (duns) always stand high on the surface film, ready to take off at any moment. Trout know this and, when food is abundant, often prefer to go for easier prey: spent insects drifting on the surface, or hatching nymphs in their final aquatic stage of metamorphosis. A hatching nymph remains just under the surface, whereas an adult insect lives above the water. For this reason, it is usually wise to choose lightly-dressed flies which fish in, rather than on, the surface film.

water warms up, activity is reduced during the middle hours of the day, picking up again at dusk.

The evening can be a magical time. Multitudes of insects are flying over the water and dropping to the surface. Drawn by such easy prey, the fish station themselves in the stream in large numbers. The party is just about to begin in earnest.

For a big catch, the best method is to take up position by a pool where it is possible to cast easily without too much moving around. There is no point in making things more difficult than necessary. The trout lose their habitual wariness and you can go on catching fish until it is quite dark. Such moments, rare though they be, more than make up for the lean times.

In the high summer months of July and August, the water is too warm and trout are out and about only at night and in the early morning. Fly fishing is less rewarding and at this time of year it is best to try natural insect baits. The trout leave the main stream and take up station close to the bank, under branches and overhanging clumps of grass. The fish are patrolling just below the surface, so you need to be careful. But if a clumsy insect falls in, you can be sure they will gratefully accept it.

When fishing with insects baits, take them by surprise

Surprise is an important factor. Never drop your insect in front of a trout's nose, which would give it time to study the bait and become aware of the deception. Land you grasshopper behind the fish, letting it drop from a height. And do not respond to a violent take with an equally brutal strike. Your leader needs to be fine (12 or 14/100ths at the most) and could easily break. A natural fly is one of the best summer-time trout baits. First you need to find some. There are two possible methods: take the trouble to catch some house flies (they are rather small but quite acceptable to trout), or raise some yourself from maggots bought from a tackle dealer. Do not expose them to sunlight to speed up the process: they would die in a few hours. When the flies hatch out, the most difficult part of the operation is to transfer them to your tackle box. The trick is to cover the cage and let daylight shine in through a small opening leading to the box. The flies should make their way to the light without any fuss.

Grasshoppers are best collected at dawn, when the dew is on the ground: the active insects are easier to catch when less active. Try the green, wingless variety. They are best fished sub-surface and sink better when threaded on the shank of the hook. Only calm stretches and shallow swims near the bank should be fished with a floating insect.

August: a poor month, except when it rains

August is the least favorable month of the year, especially when the weather is hot and dry, but you can take advantage of rainy days, especially the period after a storm, when the water level has risen and is falling again. Late August and September rains normally

A superb specimen of native European brown trout. There are many different varieties, but all are marked with red and black spots on their sides.

FOLLOWING PAGES *Trout about to take an artificial fly. The least error of presentation and the fish will refuse to take the lure.*

restore the trouts' appetite. Physical needs in relation to impending spawning bring the mature males and females out to feed. The responsible fisherman, concerned to conserve the wild strain in his river, will return them to the water alive. In cooler mountain regions, the migration to the headwaters will have already begun, and any swim may harbor a fine trout. Each square yard of river therefore needs to be fished with precision.

September: good sport to be had, before packing away rods in readiness for another season

Falling temperatures are a renewed stimulus to aquatic insects. You can try a wet fly, or offer a dry fly as soon as you see the fish rising again. The season is drawing to a close. Enjoy yourself, but be sure to return all fish to the water, especially the females. They are easily recognized by their thicker bodies and shorter heads. The males are beginning to develop an elongated lower jaw, or "kype."

Just as the indigenous rainbow trout in the USA has a migratory form (steelhead) which spends a juvenile period in freshwater and then a period at sea feeding, returning to freshwater for spawning purposes, there is an equivalent in Europe of the brown trout. This migratory form of the brown trout is termed "sea trout" and is to be encountered from the Scandinavian countries as far south as the Mediterranean although it is more adapted to the cooler, northern areas where frequency and sizes improve. The local names for this fish, and its young form are many and varied (e.g. sewin, peal, finnock, herling, whitling). From a European angler's viewpoint the sea trout assumes importance as a sporting quarry when it enters the river from the sea for eventual spawning purposes. This can be in early spring for larger fish in the north but the main runs will be from June in northern parts to September in Spain, which will be the limit of its temperature tolerance range. When it returns initially to fresh water from the sea, the sea trout can sometimes be easy to deceive. However, once it has been in fresh water for a period it becomes extremely shy and the best chance of success comes in the hours of darkness combined with extreme caution in the approach. The sea trout is referred to the same species, s. trutta, as brown trout, but is often accorded subspecific distinction. In France, the season ends on different dates in different localities. The authorities in mountain regions draw the line in mid-September, the others in October. Thereafter, the trout enthusiast can still fish for sea trout. They begin their journey upstream, wave after wave, starting in September. Unlike salmon, which abstain from food, these fish can be taken on natural baits, earth-worms and deadbaits, but most fishermen prefer to use lures, spoons and artificial flies. Spoons may be of the rotating or undulating type, though they should have a good long metal plate and should not pull too strongly in the fast currents preferred by these fish. When fly fishing, the technique is the same as for brown trout: comb the stream thoroughly, extending your range by 12 inches or so on each cast.

LEFT *Magic moment, as a trout slowly rises to take a mayfly.*

GLOSSARY

Able: a local variety of bleak which does not grow beyond 2 inches in length. It is found in ponds and small lakes. An excellent bait for trout.

American crayfish: this small crustacean was introduced to European rivers at the end of the last century. It has colonized many waters and is officially considered a pest. It can be used as bait for bass, and will also be taken by pike.

American minnow: a tiny member of the family Cyprinidae. In many countries, it is imported for use as a live or deadbait in place of the indigenous minnow, which is losing ground everywhere. The American import cannot reproduce naturally and does not represent the slightest threat to native fish.

Attractor rig: hookless lure designed to attract fish over a wide area and draw them toward a real bait. For zander and walleyes, shiny spoons are often used for this purpose. The fish rarely bites, but its curiosity is stimulated. For perch, shiny balls fulfill the same role.

Backing: a reserve of line – rarely more than a 100 feet except for salmon fishing – supplementing a fly line, which may be needed in the case of a really big fish. For reservoir fishing, very short, heavy fly lines (shooting heads) are used (30 to 32 feet), supplemented by backing. The backing passes more easily through the rings, facilitating a longer cast.

Bleak: a small member of the carp family (Cyprinidae), mainly a surface feeder. Its silvery scales make it a good livebait, attracting predators from far and wide. Unfortunately, it is also rather fragile, which can limit its usefulness.

Body: part of an artificial fly imitating a real insect's abdomen. It is tied with silk using different materials to achieve as lifelike an appearance as possible.

Cerci (or setae): the two or three long tails at the end of a mayfly's abdomen. When tying artificial flies, fibers from the flight feathers of a goose or cockerel are used to imitate the tails. They have the additional advantage of causing the spent mayfly to float in a more natural position.

Devon: fish-shaped or tubular lure consisting of a metal, wood or plastic body and propeller-like spinner vanes. Excellent for catching salmon, smaller versions are suitable for trout.

Ecdyonuridae: a family of large, late-season mayfly, which lives mainly in running water. When it is on the wing, in June and later, anglers imitate it with buff and gray spiders with red or maroon-colored bodies.

Ecouvillon: type of wet fly, weighted at the rear/below the body so that the fly assumes a vertical position each time the line goes slack.

Ephemeroptera: the many up-winged insects belonging to this order are recognizable by their having only one pair of fully developed wings. Their larvae (nymphs) are born in water and live an aquatic life for the first year or more. Some burrow (e.g. the mayfly larva); others swim around (Baetidae); yet others hide under stones. As they approach their final stage, they emigrate to the surface, where the adult insect emerges and begins its airborne existence. Some species pass through an intermediate stage as a subimago (or dun) and undergo a final molt before becoming a full-blown imago (or spinner). The adult insect is very short-lived, mating, laying its eggs and dying in the space of just a few hours. Fish feed on these insects at every stage of their development.

Great red sedge (Phryganea sp.): aquatic insect of the Trichoptera order resembling a moth. The artificial fly patterned on it is called a sedge.

Gregarious: living in groups. Almost all members of the carp family are gregarious, as are perch and their allies. Perch, walleyes, and large- and smallmouth bass live in shoals, though their numbers tend to diminish as the fish grow bigger. Pike are not gregarious when young, preferring a solitary existence in a territory which they defend against all comers. Salmon vary in their behavior: at sea, they are generally gregarious. Brown trout do not shoal, and vigorously defend their hunting grounds against intruders.

Gut-hooked: this is the term used when a fish swallows the hook right down. Be very careful to avoid this if you intend to release the fish after capture. It is a very real risk if you wait too long before striking. A pike tends to swallow its prey down quickly. When fishing for trout with natural bait, it is also advisable to strike at the first tug on the line.

Hackle: feathers from the neck cape of a cockerel. They are used for making the "hackle" of artificial flies, which can be made to represent wings and legs. The longer, stiffer fibers are used for tails.

Half-moon lead: a flattened weight often fixed at the head end of lures, spoons or spinners to make them move through the water at greater depth and at the same time eliminate line twist. This type of weight is most often used by salmon fishermen.

Hatch: mass emergence of adult insects. In the case of aquatic species, fish gorge themselves on the vast quantities of hapless prey. Hatches of terrestrial insects may also lead to frenzied feeding on the part of trout. Ants and some species of beetle emerge in vast numbers and tend to end up in rivers.

Keepnet: even for game fish, a keepnet is useful. Avoid metal versions, which can tear the fish's scales. British-style keepnets, made of nylon, are ideal for keeping fish, which are to be released at the end of the day's sport, secure and undamaged.

Ledgering: method of fishing with natural baits. It is a very useful technique to master as it allows the bait to be placed on the bed of deep lakes and swift-flowing rivers. The weighted line has no float and the angler feels the presence of the fish by the tug transmitted to the line, or by a bite indicator on or attached to the stationary rod.

Mayfly: large species of Ephemeroptera, common on some rivers in May and June. Trout feed on them with abandon. Sadly, the mayfly is becoming less common almost everywhere.

Palmer: general representation fly. The hackle is tapered evenly along the whole shank of the hook. A palmer is suitable for fishing disturbed waters and fast-flowing rivers.

Perlidae: large insect, which folds its wings, fan-like, over its back. It is also known as a stonefly, as it tends to take up position on large stones. Not of great interest as bait.

Pirk or Jig: weighted perch lure, used for fishing from a boat. An excellent lure when you know where the fish are stationed and can anchor in the vicinity. It also enables the angler to fish among obstacles and obstructions.

Plecoptera (stonefly): insect which, at rest, folds its wings over its back. It is also imitated by a sedge.

Plug: a wooden or plastic lure representing small fish. Of the three kinds (e.g. floating plugs, floating divers, and sinking plugs) the floating divers are the most versatile. Expert retrieving can create very lifelike actions of a "fish".

Pool: widening or deeper point in a river, where salmon tend to take up station.

Sedge: artificial fly characterized by a tuft of fibers tied along the shank of the hook in imitation of the folded wings of certain insects, particularly Trichoptera. A sedge can also be tied with bushy hackles to simulate the skimming action of an adult fly on the surface.

Spawning ground: area where fish breed. Walleyes are very aggressive when on their spawning grounds, and easy to catch. The same is true of pike. Protection from poachers is therefore vital. Fishing must be forbidden while fish are spawning.

Spider: an artificial fly, (normally wingless), designed to imitate insects of the Ephemeroptera order (mayflies), which have only one well-developed pair of wings (the second pair is rudimentary). A fully dressed spider can be fished as a floating dry fly; lightly dressed versions are used as wet flies.

Swivel: a two-piece metal component, one part of which can turn independently of the other. It is used to prevent a line from becoming twisted. A swivel is essential where a steel trace joins the main nylon line.

Trichoptera: insect with two pairs of wings which, like the Ephemeroptera, lives part of its life-cycle in water. The adult insect folds its wings triangular fashion over its back. Unlike the Plecoptera, whose wings are transparent like those of a fly, Trichoptera have colored wings, similar to moths.

Trolling: an extremely simple method of fishing. A line with a lure is cast out behind the boat. As the boat moves, the lure is pulled through the water with a regular motion. Where the law permits, this technique is most effective for taking really big pike and walleye. Plugs and spoons are the best lures for trolling, but deadbait is often highly effective.

Waders: large waterproof trousers or thigh-length boots which enable the angler to fish standing in deep water. Some clubs forbid the use of waders in the springtime, so as to protect the spawning grounds of grayling.

Wax moth larva: larva of a parasitic species of beetle found in bee-hives, sold by some specialist fishing-tackle dealers. The larvae conceal themselves in cells in corrugated cardboard. Check the condition of the insects: fresh larvae should be fat and clear-skinned, just like the may beetle grubs found in gardens.

INDEX